camp

MICHAEL D. EISNER

WARNER BOOKS

NEW YORK   BOSTON

Warner Books

Time Warner Book Group
1271 Avenue of the Americas, New York, NY 10020
Visit our Web site at www.twbookmark.com.

Printed in the United States of America

First Edition: June 2005
10   9   8   7   6   5   4   3   2

Library of Congress Cataloging-in-Publication Data
Eisner, Michael
    Camp / Michael D. Eisner. — 1st ed.
        p. cm.
    ISBN 0-446-53369-6
    1. Eisner, Michael — Childhood and youth. 2. Chief executive officers — United
States — Biography. 3. Keewaydin Camp. I. Title
    PN1998.3.E36A3 2005
    384'.8'092—dc22   2005005025

Book design by Giorgetta Bell McRee

To Waboos

Niminwenindam Kikeniminán.
(Algonquin for "I am happy to know you.")

acknowledgments

If forty years in the entertainment business have taught me one thing, it's that any creative project requires the devotion and dedication of many. This small labor of love was no different. Larry Kirshbaum at Warner Books believed in this book long before I had written its first word, and his wisdom, enthusiasm, and good humor . . . and the fact that he went to Camp Indianola in Madison, Wisconsin . . . were all appreciated along the way. Also, I want to thank Aaron Cohen for his tireless efforts in helping to bring this book to life—without him it would still be just a good idea. I want to acknowledge my three sons, who carried on the family tradition at Keewaydin and kept my love for the place alive. I also want to thank my lawyer of thirty years, Irwin Russell, for riding the currents with me. My office staff, Virginia Hough, Beth Huffman, and Dee Case, helped me track down old scrapbooks, photos, and memorabilia from my days—and my sons' days—at camp. Peter Hare and his staff at Keewaydin couldn't have been nicer, more supportive, or more accommodating. And Sandy Chivers and everyone at Keewaydin Temagami were the most gracious of hosts during our visit. But of course I want to especially thank my wife, Jane, who patiently listens to camp stories told often more than once.

AN IDEAL CAMPER MUST

Be honest and loyal
Be a fair winner and a good loser
Be modest
Enter into all activities
Always be willing to help
Avoid crabbing
Take his medicine when he deserves it
Have a clean sense of humor
Be a good mixer
Be clean in speech and habits
Be a leader
Be a good tripper
Be broad-minded
Be willing to help the other fellow

~KEEWAYDIN COUNCIL~

contents

contents

foreword

john mcphee

At Vassar College a few decades ago, I read to a gymful of
people some passages from books I had written, and then
received questions from the audience. The first person
said, "Of all the educational institutions you went to
when you were younger, which one had the greatest in-
fluence on the work you do now?" The question stopped
me for a moment because I had previously thought about
the topic only in terms of individual teachers and never
in terms of institutions. Across my mind flashed the
names of a public-school system K through 12, a New
England private school (13), and two universities—one in
the United States, one abroad—and in a split second I
blurted out, "The children's camp I went to when I was
six years old."

The response drew general laughter, but, funny or not,
it was the simple truth. As I once began a piece of writing in *The New Yorker* magazine, "I grew up in a summer
camp—Keewaydin—whose specialty was canoes and

canoe travel." It was at the north end of Lake Dunmore, about eight miles from Middlebury, in Vermont. In addition to ribs, planking, quarter-thwarts, and open gunwales, you learned to identify rocks, ferns, and trees. You played tennis. You backpacked in the Green Mountains on the Long Trail. If I were to make a list of all the varied subjects that have come up in my articles and books, adding a check mark beside interests derived from Keewaydin, most of the entries would be checked. I spent all summer every summer at Keewaydin from age six through fifteen, and later was a counselor there, leading canoe trips and teaching swimming, for three years while I was in college.

The Kicker was the name of the camp newspaper, and its editor was my first editor, a counselor named Alfred G. Hare, whose surname translated to the Algonquian Waboos, a nickname that had been with him from childhood and would ultimately stay with him through his many years as Keewaydin's director. Waboos was a great editor. He laughed in the right places, cut nothing, and let you read your pieces aloud at campfires. If this book, in its varied appreciations of Keewaydin, has a hero, he's it.

When I first arrived at Keewaydin as a child (my father was the camp's physician), the name Eisner was all over the place—on silver trophies and on the year-by-year boards in the dining hall that listed things like Best Swimmer, Best Athlete, Best Singles Canoe. The author of this book was not one of those Eisners. When I first arrived at Keewaydin, he was still pushing zero. He had five years to wait before he was born. His father, Lester, was among the storied Eisners, and so were assorted uncles and cousins. Over time, multiple Eisners would follow. In 1949, when Lester Eisner brought Michael to the camp to see if he would like to enroll there (a scene of some hilarity that you will find a few pages hence), I was in the first of my three years as a counselor in the oldest of the four age groups into which the camp was divided. In the two summers that followed (the last ones for me), he was in the youngest group and I didn't know him from Mickey Mouse. I was aware only that another Eisner had come to Keewaydin.

Summer camps have varying specialties and levels of instruction. They differ considerably in character and mission. No one description, positive or negative, can come near fitting all of them or even very many. Keewaydin was not a great experience for just anybody. My beloved publisher—Roger W. Straus, Jr., founder of Farrar, Straus & Giroux—went to Keewaydin when he was thirteen years old and hated every minute of it. That amounts to about eighty thousand minutes. Over the years, he spent at least a hundred thousand minutes making fun of me for loving Keewaydin. The probable cause was Keewaydin's educational rigor. Gently but firmly, you were led into a range of activity that left you at the end of the summer with enhanced physical skills and knowledge of the natural world. You wanted to go back, and back. Mike Eisner went back in 2000 (hardly for the first or last time). He was fifty-eight. Keewaydin was celebrating the career of its eighty-five-year-old emeritus director. Three people spoke at a Saturday night campfire. Each was introduced only by name, with no mention of any business or profession or affiliation, just, in turn, Peter Hare, Russ MacDonald, Mike Eisner. In his blue jeans and ball cap, walking around the flames with his arms waving, Eisner told three hundred pre-teen and early-teen-aged kids escalating stories of his own days at Keewaydin. They listened closely and laughed often. Few, if any, knew who else he was.

prologue

it all started at a knicks game

New York, Madison Square Garden, courtside, 2001. The Knicks against the Pacers. The score was tied, and halftime was about to end.

I could sense that I was about to be approached by a stranger. His intent, I assumed, was to offer a comment about a new ride at Disney World or hand me a movie script.

Instead, he gave me a card identifying himself as George Stein, head of the Tri-State Camping Conference. Above the noise of an impatient crowd as the second half began, he said he'd heard I was an enthusiast of summer camp. His group was holding an annual conference and wanted me to speak about my experiences. Without hesitation, I said, "yes." The word *camp* had taken away my usual reflex to slow things down and come up with a polite no.

Sitting next to me was my oldest friend, John Angelo. He looked at me quizzically. "I thought you only speak at colleges where one of your sons is applying," he said. "True," I replied, "but this is about camp, after all." As I turned my attention back to the game, and Reggie Miller sank a three-point shot, I was already thinking about what I'd say at the conference.

My family has been attending Camp Keewaydin in Salisbury, Vermont, for over eighty years. I started at age eight and finished as a "staffman" when I was twenty-two, a recent college graduate. The next summer, I entered the television and movie world as an usher at NBC. Keewaydin is a hiking and canoeing camp, with a dual focus on the wilderness trips campers take each summer and in-camp activities like sports, all guided by a low-key philosophy with an emphasis on self-improvement within a framework of group accomplishment. To this day, I fondly recall the challenges of building a fire, pitching a tent, climbing a New England mountain, canoeing on a lake. Camp songs still resonate inside me. Competition exists at Keewaydin, of course, but nobody fails summer camp, a nice respite from winters of fortune and misfortune at school.

To the uninitiated, camp may sound like one grandiose cliché—teamwork, brotherhood, helping the other guy. But clichés are often constructed on truths from the past. Away from the modern comforts and parental safety of home, summer camp may seem like boot camp to some, with its lack of privacy, wilderness rituals, mosquito bites, freezing lake water, tent clean-ups, and canoe portages (carrying your canoe over land). When you've been a camper, though, the planned deprivations are fun, exciting, the stuff from which character is built. As I've gotten older, they make more and more sense. Camp taught me a lot of little things, and the experiences accumulated into some

prologue

big "stuff," stuff that builds backbone and teaches lessons that keep popping up in adulthood.

At first, writing the camp speech was purely recreation, something very different from my usual routines at investor conferences or annual meetings, at story conferences or production meetings. Then, as I started to put words on paper, a funny transformation took place. I realized this simple idea of institutionalized fun was much more serious than I had originally thought. For me, camp really mattered.

I gave the speech to a surprise standing ovation (my first and only, I think), and afterward continued prodding my camp memories. I have always thought that those who spend too much time reflecting on the past aren't focusing enough on the present or future, but in those times, it was a welcome escape from the chaos. Around me, the world was changing, due to the September 11, 2001, attacks on American soil in New York City and Washington, D.C., and the war on terror that followed. In my business life, a weakened economy and personal vendettas exceptional even by Hollywood standards led to shareholder discontent and crises in the boardroom. Just as physical exercise so often proves to release consuming tensions, the mental exercise of reflecting on camp, doing a bit of writing early each morning or late each night, made it all seem a bit easier, if only for a moment here or there.

For everybody, life at the beginning of the twenty-first century was tenuous and complicated, and we all looked for strength in different places. Family, religion, friends, childhood institutions—the entire structure of one's past factors into the fiber that holds us together. For me

prologue

summer camp was part of that bond. It was this world that had taught me that if you maintain faith in your values and knowledge, and stay true to yourself, the bears in the woods will eventually disappear. The Alan Menken and David Zippel song from Disney's animated movie *Hercules* could be a camp song written after a rainy and windy wilderness trip. As one of the lines goes, "And I won't look back, I can go the distance and I'll stay on track; No, I won't accept defeat." I realized that I had developed my values and knowledge at summer camp. Many of my principles were Keewaydin principles.

My speech at the camping conference jump-started a family goal: My children have long wanted to share our actual camping experiences with other kids who might be less fortunate and would never have the opportunity for camping. This notion jelled with Keewaydin's growing desire to foster diversity among its campers. Three years ago, my wife Jane and I, and my three sons, Breck, Eric, and Anders, were able through our family foundation to send promising kids from less advantaged backgrounds in California to camp—boys to Keewaydin and girls to its sister camp, Songadeewin. In this book, I describe some of the experiences of the Southern Californian boys and how camp changed their lives, just as it changed the lives of all the Eisners.

Thinking more about Keewaydin, and getting involved with the camp again, I found myself wanting to learn more

prologue

about the institution. Most important, I wanted to reconnect with Keewaydin's greatest teacher, Alfred Hare, better known as Waboos, a boy from Philadelphia who started at camp with my father when he was eight in 1923, who became the camp director in 1945, and who is still there today, over eight decades later, a guiding spirit of American camping.

In some ways, I've been working on this book for fifty-six years, ever since my first night at Keewaydin. In other ways, it's been a labor of love for the past three years, completed largely on my laptop computer in spare moments. A few times, the project was put on the back burner by distractions from people who could have used a few summers at camp earlier in their lives, but as on any Keewaydin trip, I never lost faith or focus that it would be completed. It only seems appropriate that, after such a tumultuous few years, I can produce a response that has nothing to do with Hollywood antics or boardroom politics, but everything to do with the experience you need to survive them.

When I decided to write this book, I decided I needed a researcher and editor—a good bowman, in canoe-speak—to get it done right. I found a young writer and television producer named Aaron Cohen. I had read an essay he had written about watching his beloved New York Mets play each year on his birthday, all the way back to when he was in the second grade. That appealed to me. Aaron became my eyes and ears at the camp when I couldn't be there. He observed some of what you'll read about in this book. In the interest of simplicity, we've combined our voices.

prologue

Yes, this book is a valentine to summer camp, but it also contains, I hope, the answers to questions that have vexed me since I started writing the speech about camping. Why does summer camp matter as an institution, and why is it so important?

Let's start at the beginning.

camp

chapter one

the first trip

1949

It was the summer of 1949, and I was seven. Some forty miles north of New York City, my family had a summer home on sixty acres, "in the back" (as we called it) of my grandfather's gentleman's farm. I was attending a day camp, Camp Mohawk, to do what kids in Bedford Hills and Mount Kisco and Chappaqua and Armonk and White Plains did when their parents wanted every minute accounted for during the summer. I had been at Mohawk just one week, already the survivor of a lost baseball mitt and my sister's throwing up in the bus, when the subject of overnight camp came up.

We were sitting at dinner on the screened porch of the house when the voice of God (God was my father) said, "I thought I'd take you up to Camp Keewaydin to see if you might want to go there next summer."

I was excited and paralyzed. As far as I can now remember, I had never gone on an overnight trip with my father alone, without a sister or mother. He was a father I called by his first name, Lester. Yes, he was my real father, and no, I cannot imagine why he liked that. They said it was because my sister couldn't say "Daddy," but I doubt it. For much of the first three years of my life, he had been flying planes in the "war" (World War II), and, since then, had remained the man who inspired enduring respect, love, admiration, envy, and fear, and all that was fatherhood to me.

My father was a man of adventure. After the war, he had started an airline in Ecuador that he scraped together from two army air force planes. Flying to South America with your father as the pilot was certainly an adventure. But then he had settled down as a lawyer in the world of New York City. Surely everyone thinks their father is unique, and at a young age, the impression I had of my father was no different. He was athletic, a bold entrepreneur, clever humorist, attentive husband, matinee idol to my sister's friends and simply bigger than life to my friends. The women loved him, and children were awed by him. As a seven-year-old, I saw all this, and was at once respectful and impressed and mesmerized and sometimes daunted by his power.

The prospect of sleepaway camp was a family tradition that he would not let drop. So, we were scheduled to do this "father-son" thing and go off for the weekend to Kee-waydin, a summer camp that my father and uncles had attended. I sat at the dinner table contemplating the many hours in the car where I'd be alone with my father, wondering about the camp in the middle of nowhere, amid millions and millions of acres of woods, billions and billions of miles from Bedford Hills, without a sister or mother in sight.

Memories of the trip up are hazy. I'm sure my father explained to me that this was a great camp, and shared some of the happy memories he had of going up to Vermont each summer. We headed in our Buick toward New England. We probably drove up Route 7 in Vermont until we passed Brandon, then made a right toward Salisbury and drove onward on Route 53 to Keewaydin. I do remember that it was dark when we arrived, and I was nervous. Placed inside a sleeping bag, I slept on a cot, within some sort of dark enclosure, and I fell asleep wondering what it looked like outside. My father had disappeared.

The next morning, a loud alien gong noise greeted me with the morning light. I found myself in a tent with wooden floors, surrounded by boys my own age, who were getting out of their beds, looking at me with the persistent, perplexing glare that boys are prone to adopt toward a stranger. I stared back with a matching glare of my own, though Mother Nature soon took over, and a critical question flooded my mind: Where's the bathroom? I was painfully in need of one; somehow, bathroom emergencies at seven are at least doubly more painful than most men remember. I stumbled out of bed and followed the scattering of boys scurrying away to a community john that was two dirt basketball courts away, and then followed the crowd to the dining hall, seemingly half a mile down some kind of path. A staffman discovered me wandering and connected me with my father, a lone familiar face among hundreds.

I was introduced to several adults, most notably someone called Waboos (or at least it was pronounced that way—WAH-boos). His importance was underscored not only by his unique name but by the fact that nearly every youngster and adult who walked by made a point of saying, "Good morning, Waboos," a greeting he returned. Among all the old folks whom I was introduced to, Waboos was clearly the featured attraction, and, furthermore, he called my father "Les." I never had heard that. Everybody called him by his full name, Lester. I knew this was a special relationship. This was someone from my father's past.

The rest of the day was peppered with activity. I was shipped back to the group of kids with whom I had spent the night. I folded my sleeping bag while everybody else made their beds. I washed my face and brushed my teeth alongside twenty other boys also brushing away, quite a change from sharing a bathroom with just one sister.

I played, I swam, I rested, then played and swam again with the boys for the rest of the day. I didn't see my father again until dinner, when I spotted him huddled with Waboos, talking, as the two of them looked over at me. Maybe I had embarrassed my father. Maybe I had offended the other kids. Something was off—I knew it. Waboos approached me.

"Do you want to box tonight?" he asked. I heard myself say, "Sure," not having any idea what he was talking about. It turned out that I was headed to the weekly Saturday-evening wrestling and boxing show at Sunset Arena, the old ring beyond right-center field on one of the Keewaydin ball fields. Each age group of campers (wig-wams, I was learning to call them) presented four events—two wrestling, two boxing. The more I learned, the more I hoped my mother would somehow appear to get me out of all of it. Suddenly, this father-son thing definitely wasn't working.

The youngest kid at the camp was eight; I was seven. The opponent that I was picked to fight had been in camp from day one, was totally confident, and I'm sure later went on to be a successful fullback in the NFL. He, in fact, was nine, and here on my first full day at Kee-waydin, I was matched up against him, in the ring, mano a mano.

The fight that night lasted about two minutes. I didn't cry, I didn't take a dive. Even though the oversized gloves were like pillows, I had the stuffing and pride beaten out of me—not necessarily in that order. After what I'm sure was some encouragement bestowed upon me by Waboos and my father, we left the camp for the drive back to Bed-ford Hills.

I slept the whole way home. I only opened my eyes as my father carried me upstairs to my real bed. I woke up as he tripped slightly on the stairs; my mother was right be-hind us.

"You should have seen how brave he was," I heard my father saying to my mother. "He was a stand-up boy."

"Isn't Waboos a great guy?" he said to me, curled up in his arms. "Don't you want to go to Keewaydin next summer?"

"Yeah," I mumbled, and fell back to sleep before we made it to my bed.

chapter two

a return to roots

present

Over a half century later, on the day before camp begins, I'm heading south from downtown Middlebury on Route 7 for what seems like the thousandth time. The scenery turns to farmland, cows grazing in fields alongside the road. Eventually, I spot a sign for Lake Dunmore and turn my rental car onto Route 153, leading past a cluster of vacation homes and then without fanfare (and only a small sign), we are facing a large ball field. To the south of the field is the lake. On the north side is the dining hall; on the east side, a few camp offices; and to the west and beyond are several *Waramaug* tents for younger campers (I lived in Tent 10 in 1951). Nearby, sticking out a bit awkwardly, is a small one-room cottage with two steps leading to its entrance.

On the walls inside the cottage is a smorgasbord of photographs of Keewaydin personalities, some in black and white, some in color. All the pictures are accompanied by short typewritten paragraphs, cut out and glued to the bottom of the portrait, describing the individual in the picture and his accomplishments at camp. These are pictures that tell the history of Keewaydin.

A man—now approaching ninety—is sitting in this cottage on the edge of the ball field less than fifty yards from the lake. It's the ageless Waboos. This summer, he'll spend much of the day behind his desk, sitting, chatting, napping, chatting again, dozing again. It's a comfortable pattern, but for someone who cannot see two feet in front of him, and who is always considerably less mobile than he was in previous years, it's very confining.

His immobility almost prevented him from being at camp this summer, or at least sleeping at camp. How could he be expected to walk at night? How could anyone navigate the hidden rocks, sinuous tree roots, or slippery patches of wet grass that could quickly lead to a broken hand, or hip, or worse?

Right now, the day before camp starts, he is back for the summer; after all these years, really, how could they keep him away from a place that gives him life? "Tomorrow is the beginning of the world," he says, his face suddenly animated as he contemplates the first day of camp. He is sitting behind the desk, looking at photos on a machine that illuminates and enlarges them. Doesn't really help too much, he says to visitors with a slightly embarrassed and helpless look. Once in the morning and once in the afternoon each day, he'll rise from the desk and take his memorized paces out of the cottage, moving carefully down the two steps. One foot in front of the other, slowly, deliberately, ducklike, he walks along the lake, across the field,

right through a game going on as he heads to the fort—
the Keewaydin term for bathroom. The campers will turn
and take note, most offering hellos. He'll turn and acknowledge the greetings to the outlines of shadows that he
can barely make out.

Back in the cottage, this eight-by-ten-foot Keewaydin
museum, he sorts through various old binders, postcards,
and notebooks. Each reveals some piece of the camp's past.
In one high corner of the wall behind him, there is a missing spot where an aged picture used to hang: smiling boys,
eight, nine, and ten years old, standing naked on a rock
along a racing river, the "cascades," captured after a long
hike by a long-forgotten photographer. My father and this
man in the cottage were among the boys. But the picture
is gone.

The pile of old binders on a side table contains scattered
old *Kickers*, or weekly wrap-ups of Keewaydin news.
They're where John McPhee took the first insightful and
humorous steps in his literary career. On the hut's slanted
ceiling hang four wooden boards, representing the four
wigwams, each chronicling the course of their respective
leadership, and with that, more of the camp's history. Peter
Hare is listed as *Wiantinaug*'s director, 1987–1997. I still
have trouble getting over the fact that Peter, now the
camp's director, is no longer in diapers.

The cottage smells old and musty, but in a real, active,
used way. This is the old man's space.

I greet him warmly, and pepper him with questions. How did he get that name? Who names someone Waboos?

It's a story that's rooted in the very history of American summer camping. In 1923, an eight-year-old boy named Alfred Hare had come for his first summer at camp, a year before my father's arrival. A business partner of Alfred's father had sent his kids to camp, and it seems that the Hares decided their son would benefit from such an experience as well. His mother took him up to Grand Central Station in New York from their home in Philadelphia, before putting him on the train to New England with other boys headed to camp. Despite some protestations typical of an eight-year-old, little Alfie was off to the first of eight decades of summers at Keewaydin.

In the 1920s, summer camps and programs were not as widespread as they are today in the United States. (According to the American Camping Association, more than 10 million youngsters now attend some type of camp each summer.) Organized camping began back in the summer of 1861, when a school headmaster named Frederick Gunn took a group of his pupils into the rocky Connecticut wilderness with the idea that experience in nature and the outdoors—the hiking, camping, cooking, and so forth—could lead to character building and emotional growth. The idea took, and over the next half-century, permanent summer camps began to pop up around New England and the Northeast.

One of Frederick Gunn's campers, A. S. Gregg Clarke, decided in 1893 against a career in law and instead set out to start his own summer camp modeled after his mentor's ideas. "Commodore" Clarke, as he was affectionately known, eventually settled on a permanent home for his camp in northern Ontario, on an island on the north side of Lake Temagami. The area was populated only by Indians and accessible only by canoe. He named the camp Keewaydin, an Ojibway Indian word from the Longfellow poem *Hiawatha*, literally meaning the northwest wind, which was a harbinger of good weather and fair tripping—an Indian omen of good luck. The camp was successful, and in 1910, the Commodore opened a second Keewaydin camp in Salisbury, Vermont, on Lake Dunmore. Years later, when I arrived there as a camper, Dunmore felt to me, a boy from New York, as far away and uninhabited as any place could be.

The camp prospered, and thirteen years after it opened, Alfred Hare arrived at Dunmore. As is still the case today, staffmen (the Keewaydin word for counselors) and campers rotated around the dining-hall tables each week, mixing and matching with old friends, finding new ones. The camp director was a man they called Major Gunn, and one week, Alfred was placed at his table. As the youngsters took turns introducing themselves, the young blond— almost white-haired—boy greeted the director and told him his name.

"Hare, eh?" the major said. "Well, from now on, we're going to call you Waboos. It means 'white rabbit' in Algonquin. Waboos is your new name here."

The camp looks pretty much the same today—the same large trees, the same air to breathe, that same lake smell— all the same as the start of summer in 1949, when my father took me there, and even in 1924, when my father originally came to Keewaydin. He was sent because of an untimely death—his mother's. The cause of death was appendicitis, though the captain of a ship sailing from Cuba to Florida originally misdiagnosed it as simple seasickness. My father was the eldest of the three Eisner boys suddenly without a mother, and at some point in the months following, my father's father, also named Lester, decided that his ten-year-old son would benefit from spending the summer at a camp in Vermont. The devastation my father felt from losing his mother must have been horrific. (I still recall the relief of passing the age of ten, and knowing my mother was just fine.)

Probably still in shock from the death of his mother, my father hated his first summer at camp, or so my uncle Gerald now tells me. But he went back, and back again, and his younger brothers, Gerald and Jacques, would join him at Keewaydin a few summers later. Keewaydin had been founded as a combination tripping and "liberal arts" camp, and then, as it does now, provided a little bit of everything for everyone. Campers went on several overnight canoe trips each summer, but they also spent time on campus, swimming, playing sports, doing arts and crafts, getting a rounded camp education. While my father and Uncle Gerald enjoyed the sporting aspects of Keewaydin's program, my uncle Jacques preferred other activities, like oil painting and crafts. I'm particularly struck by this because the youngest of my own three sons, Anders (who in the winter was a great ice hockey player), pursued more artistic activities at camp.

My father never talked about his difficult first summer; instead, all I ever heard from him was his love for and dedication to Keewaydin, a dedication that bordered on the religious. It was a passion for nature and the outdoors, and a love of the institution and its people. He frequently passed up high school, college, and law school reunions, but my father never missed a Keewaydin reunion. He had gone to Princeton as an undergraduate and then to Harvard Law School, but he rarely talked of his time there. Keewaydin seemed to be his true pillar of education.

After my father's time as a camper was up, he became a junior staffman, only to be fired one summer when he was caught on the lake in a canoe with a girl. How he found a girl in what was then completely isolated rural Vermont, I'll never know. You can understand how this firing made my father a hero among my friends. Luckily, Keewaydin's director at the time, Sid Negus, invited him back the following summer, and, as I saw, everyone seemed happy to see him when he returned with his own son in 1949.

I came back that next summer, 1950, and luckily, I loved the camp, too. Reflecting upon it, I realize that my father was smart enough to downplay how much he wanted me to love the place, sensing a kind of independence brewing in me. Once I had learned to love the outdoors, and the tripping and the canoeing, as well as the sports and the camaraderie of camp life, he confessed how pleased it made him. I continued to follow in my father's footsteps when I returned to Keewaydin as a staffman after my days as a camper were complete. I loved everything about the place—if it didn't define me, I wanted it to.

A few years after my final summer, working as an ABC executive (well, more like a factotum), I took a girl I had been dating in New York, Jane Breckenridge, to the wilderness to see if we were compatible (or at least that was some of the motivation). I was going to show Jane how great the wild was. The wild, though, didn't cooperate at first, offering two nights of cold and rain and mosquitoes. Finally, on the third night, the skies cleared, and I got a fire going to make some silver cake, a specialty I first learned to make on Cupsupetic Lake in Maine. If I couldn't impress her as a hiker, maybe I could dazzle her with some cooking. We were tired, but the fresh smell of rain, combined with the aura of a beautiful Swedish-American woman, along with the isolation and opportunity that the woods presented, filled my mind with something other than silver cake. I set out a single sleeping bag under Jane's amused eye. I started cutting the cake. I looked up, and she was pointing, speechless, across the campsite. I turned around and saw a huge shadow. There was a bear big enough to impress Faulkner lurking outside our lean-to, sniffing and pawing.

Thus began the longest night of my life. Jane remained more composed and practical than I was, staying awake, keeping the fire going, and outwitting our unwanted visitor by hitting pots and pans to scare him away until the sun came up. She never cowered or complained. Thirty-seven years later, I'm still listening to that brave woman, Jane, now my wife, and her calm assessment of whatever wilderness or jungles we have found ourselves in at various points in time.

In 1979, our eldest son, Breck, became the third generation of Eisners to go to Keewaydin. And our two younger sons, Eric and Anders, followed him up to Salisbury a few years later. All of them went along the same course, moving through the wigwams, or age-based units of Keewaydin. The youngest boys, usually eight or nine years old, are in the *Annwi* wigwam. The ten- and eleven-year-olds are in *Waramaug,* and twelve- and thirteen-year-olds in *Wiantinaug,* and the oldest boys, fourteen and fifteen, in *Moosalamoo.* At the time when Anders left Keewaydin, a little over a decade ago, the camp had changed little from the place it was when my father was sent there as a ten-year-old in the early 1920s, or when I was there in the 1950s. The same tents that we had slept in now housed my sons; the same dining hall we had eaten in still fed them; and the same Waboos—once a boy, then a man, and now an elder sage—still remained a reliable and valuable fixture on the campus.

On my way to camp these many years later, I had told myself that I wanted to ask Waboos about the ethics and ideals of the camp. Instead, once inside his cottage, I find myself asking about memories and stories. I find myself asking him about my father.

In response, I get stories of baseball games, swimming in

the lake, and canoe trips through the New England wilderness. I hear about high jinks in the dining hall and sleeping outside in tents. He laughs when I ask for more details about my father getting caught with a girl in a canoe. These details, unfortunately, Waboos doesn't seem eager to provide. The talk demonstrates something rare: a dramatic steadiness through eighty years of an institution. These days, it's hard to find something that has remained the same for a decade. At Keewaydin, as I talk to Waboos, it's clear to me how much has stayed the same, and how important that is.

When I tell him I'm curious to find out my father's exact years at camp, Waboos points to some small file boxes on a lower shelf in the back corner of the space. Dusting them off, I open the first one, and he instructs me to go to the *E*'s. In a remarkable display of diligence and organization, the boxes represent a catalog of nearly every camper who came to Keewaydin during his time as head of camp and before. "Every camper?" I exclaim. "That's almost sixty years."

"Well, they haven't updated it in a few years, not since they got computers. Now they can just punch a button and . . ."

"Anders, Breck, Eric, Gerald . . ." I read aloud—the Eisners at Keewaydin, in alphabetical order. For each of my sons, it gives their years at camp, our home address, the tuition we paid. Cousins and nephews as well. On my father's card, the information is vague and incomplete, since Waboos didn't become director until 1945.

camp

When you navigate the surface of camp, the soft dirt and pebble ground that makes up so much of this place, there is a unique sound, a sound that I know, that my sons know, and my father knew. My family's history, its story, is wound tightly in this root and rock Vermont landscape. In my first summer as a camper, 1950, the year after my visit with my father, I was eight, and a member of the *Annwi* wigwam. This time, the trip to camp was an overnight train to Rutland and then an hour bus ride. I was in a pack of children until I was placed in the tent of a staffman named Dave Flight with four other kids. Dave was probably in his twenties, and yet to me, he seemed ancient, as all adults do to an eight-year-old.

A summer at Keewaydin in 1950 was an eight-week stay, with only a single parental visit in the middle. I wasn't homesick and didn't wet my bed, a definite accomplishment. My mother would write me endless letters about her friends and activities. Most of these I would place unread in the cubby next to my cot. Of course she would find the unopened letters and complain about them for the next fifty years.

That summer, we spent four weeks in one tent with Dave Flight, and then four weeks in an *Annwi* cabin with another staffman; they moved us at midseason for a change of scenery. Memories from the summer of 1950 are vivid, like many things from the distant past, clearer than details from six months ago: images of my first camping trip, the

Annwi communal shower (thankfully no longer there), writing letters home, games of Capture the Flag, visiting Fort Ticonderoga. I can almost travel back in time, back to the campfires, the fireflies and horseflies. Horseflies especially.

The single strongest memory from that first summer, though—the memory that always comes to mind in a reliable instant—is the war story Dave Flight read to us every night that first month, using his flashlight after the lights went out.

It took place in France, during the Allied invasion of Europe. For once in my life, I looked forward to bedtime. I remember the excitement I felt hearing that story, so precise in its conveyance of aircraft, soldier, and battle images. I thought of my friend John Angelo's father, who had been killed in World War II. And I also thought of Jacques Eisner, my father's brother, who had died on November 13, 1942, in the Battle of Guadalcanal.

I really only knew Jacques (pronounced "Jack") through Keewaydin. In the camp offices, right along Keewaydin Road at the front of the camp, there was "the Jacques Eisner Fireplace," donated by my grandfather. I realized even then how connected my family was to Keewaydin, but as an eight-year-old, I knew little about World War II. I didn't really know about the Germans and Hitler or the Japanese except for mentions in books like the one Dave Flight read to us.

My father always became pensive when my mother talked about Pearl Harbor, the Pacific, or the USS *San Francisco* and Jacques. The details of Jacques's death were never really known.

Dave Flight continued with the war story each night, making advances in the plot bit by bit. But then came mid-season, and I moved from my tent into the cabin, while Dave Flight—and the war story—stayed behind. The three heroes of the story had been parachuting into France, jumping out of their plane, when I moved out.

For me, those three parachuters are still in the air. But as somebody who loves stories, I've filled in my own endings hundreds of times, while waiting to find out the true course the author intended. Dave Flight lives near camp over fifty years later, and I've enlisted his daughter Ellen, who works at Keewaydin, to ask her father for help in solving the plot. He, unfortunately, has long forgotten the ending, not to mention where he placed the book after that summer.

For me, though, that story remains inside. I haven't forgotten.

chapter three

a million miles

present

While I'm at camp, catching up with Waboos and other old Keewaydin friends, the sun is just rising over Southern California, and two boys, whose names are Pepe and Quenton, are being picked up from their homes in Orange County. These are not the kind of inner-city homes you see on television in the area; these are, rather, the ones you don't see. Southern Californian neighborhoods are green. Pepe's street in Anaheim, not more than a few miles from Disneyland, looks like a pretty ordinary block: The grass is green and the trees are green. But when you take a closer look, you'll see that the kids huddled in circles on the sidewalk don't look that friendly—teenage drug dealers and gang members usually don't. And Pepe's family's apartment in the small housing complex at the end of the street is sparsely furnished, despite the fact that an entire extended family of up to a dozen people lives there. Quenton lives fifteen minutes away, on a similar block in Fullerton. It's a bit quieter, and there's probably less trouble lurking nearby, but that's only because Quenton's mother recently moved the family to this calmer area.

The boys are picked up to start their journey from California to camp by my eldest son, Breck, along with two young girls, Noelle and Veronica, going to Songadeewin of Keewaydin, the girls camp across the lake run by Dave Flight's daughter Ellen. We found Pepe and Quenton through an after-school program our company sponsors, Disney GOALS, and we located Noelle and Veronica through another organization, Project GRAD. For all the kids, it's their first plane ride, from Los Angeles to Washington, D.C., five hours in the air. Stretched along one of the plane's back rows, they record the experience with their newest toys, disposable cameras.

After a layover, they take another flight, this time going north, to Burlington, Vermont. I get to the airport early to meet them. When the kids walk off the plane, they have that familiar look of drained invigoration—the same look my sons had when we'd get to a vacation destination after a long trip.

An hour's drive, south now, is next, with Pepe and Quenton piling in one car with Breck, and the girls hopping in my car. The boys lean out of their seats for a first-ever glimpse of grazing cows, and pepper Breck, sitting in the front seat, with questions about camp. Dinner with the new campers, Breck insists, has to be at the A&W, right on Route 7, halfway between the Middlebury Inn and the turnoff to Lake Dunmore. It's where every summer, the night before camp, my wife Jane and I took our sons for a big precamp meal. Newly renovated but with the traditional roller-skating waitresses, the A&W delivers as always. The campers eagerly consume hamburgers, fries, the patented root beer float, and a giant shared banana split. (I stick with the surprisingly edible veggie burger, no mayo.)

Breck (getting used to cramped quarters before he heads off to Morocco to shoot his first movie, *Sahara*) shares a room with Pepe and Quenton, and reports the next morning that they slept quite well, after testing out their long-jumping prowess between the beds. Breakfast at the Middlebury Inn is the last bit of noncamp food for a while, and after stopping at Songadeewin to drop off the girls, we are in the Keewaydin parking lot on this opening day, with two new campers in tow.

The kids are placed in the *Waramaug* unit, the second-youngest group of campers—roughly, ages ten and eleven. A staffman helps Pepe unpack in his tent, Breck gives Quenton a hand in his tent, and I shuttle back and forth between the two, coming out of retirement to snap pictures, offer advice, and micromanage the sock cubby.

Both boys are small, but Pepe is definitely the smaller of the two. Though nearly a teenager, he stands less than four feet tall, and is very skinny, his arms like pipe cleaners, his legs like twigs. It's clear from the little time I've spent with him that he doesn't let his small size stop him. Dave Wilk, who runs the Disney GOALS program and who recommended Pepe and Quenton for summer camp, assured us that he's a scrapper, a kid who will rise to a challenge. (The GOALS program recruits disadvantaged youth in Orange County, like Pepe and Quenton, to play in an organized ice hockey league, and also acts as an afterschool program to help structure their lives.) Pepe is deceptively strong (insisting on carrying his huge backpack across *Waramaug* field) and eagerly embracing this strange new world.

As he finishes unpacking, I take Pepe over to the old man's cottage. Waboos asks the new camper his standard set of questions: "Where are you from? What wigwam are you in? Are you excited about camp?" Though he doesn't know exactly who this ancient man in front of him is, Pepe answers each question with the reverence one might reserve for royalty.

Back by his cot, as Pepe is working hard to make his bed neatly, the staffman in the tent, Cameron MacDonald, announces that swim tests are beginning. Pepe begins rummaging through his newly stacked shelves of clothes for his bathing suit. Next comes sunscreen, which he sloppily applies in record time, leaving traces of white cream on his cheeks. No matter, as he runs off to the swimming dock and takes his place among the other boys.

José Luis "Pepe" Molina is three thousand miles from his home in Anaheim, California, and it might as well be a million. I'm now watching him from afar as he stands on one end of Keewaydin's lakefront docks, next to three other boys his age, all significantly taller and chunkier than the stick-figured Pepe. The four youngsters are about to jump into the water for the same swim test my father and I and my sons took, consisting of a 150-yard potpourri of strokes—take your pick: crawl, backstroke, dog paddle—to the opposite dock. Pepe just met the other three boys a few minutes ago, and you can see the four of them, awaiting instruction and nervously babbling as anxious young boys will do in such moments of anticipation. Right now, it doesn't matter that these boys probably live in large houses in northeastern suburbs, while Pepe lives in a cramped apartment in Southern California. Here, at camp, all focus on the task at hand: They will closely trail a canoe for the balance of their swim, with one lifeguard paddling the canoe and another keeping a watchful eye on the swimmers, equipped with a pole that the boys can grab hold of if they run out of gas, out of courage, or both.

For Pepe, I think to myself, it is a time of firsts. It is his first time this far away from home. It is his first time seeing a lake, forget about swimming in one. Tonight, for the first time, he will sleep in a tent, less than twenty feet from the shoreline of the lake. For the first time, he'll know exactly where to go for his three meals per day without concern. And for the first time since moving from Mexico back to California a few years ago, he won't have to translate the English spoken around him into Spanish for his mother, who works the night shift in a factory to provide for her son. Pepe Molina is at summer camp, a million miles away from home.

He jumps in the water. For the untrained, it's a long swim, the first of many challenges of the summer, an entrée to Keewaydin that thousands of young boys have taken and passed. And passing the swim test is the ticket to general swim, immediate instruction in the canoe (to begin this afternoon), and permission even to try a kayak tomorrow. This is the kickoff to a summer of fun.

Pepe fails the swim test.

About halfway through, I see him begin to falter, to lose

steam and stamina, and the staffman in the canoe grabs his
arms and helps him up into the boat. The other campers—
larger, stronger—get across and pass, but it seems that Pepe
will have to wait for another try. The staffman will tell me
later that Pepe complained that the canoe slowed him
down, that he needed to be able to go fast and was prevented from doing so. No one else complains of this problem, though, especially no one who is able to help himself
out of the water on the other side of the lake.

Thinking about it as I return home to California on the
plane, later in the day, the situation reminds me of my own
inauspicious debut at Keewaydin more than fifty years ago,
in the boxing ring. I overcame my embarrassment, and my
failure, and now I find myself wondering if Pepe will be
able to do the same.

chapter four

traditionese

present

It's now later in the week, the first week of summer camp, and Pepe stands in left field of *Waramaug* ball field. He's got his glove on his left hand, looking into the infield as his team's pitcher delivers a thirty-mile-an-hour fastball for a strike. Pepe's been at camp for nearly a week, and despite some early jitters, he's starting to settle in.

Though Pepe's background displays a marked difference from that of most of his fellow campers—most are white and from the suburbs—his experience so far has been pretty typical of a first-time *Waramaug* camper. First things first: After a few tries, he passed the swim test, his waterfront initiation finally completed. He spent the first few days taking things in from a distance, joining in activities enthusiastically at times and hanging back a bit more fearfully at others. Little by little over these first few days, though, things have begun to click for Pepe. Soccer and basketball have quickly become his favorites. Despite his small size—when he dribbles a basketball, it looks like an

NBA point guard dribbling a large beach ball—he is a good athlete, and at times viciously competitive.

Pepe, now crouching in the outfield, hands on his knees, waiting for the ball to come his way, is getting pretty comfortable at Keewaydin. Perhaps most striking is the fact that he's starting to use the language, proudly proclaiming his membership in the *Waramaug* wigwam; smiling when staffmen greet him with the "Kway, kway" hello of Keewaydin. He even tells his staffman that he's going to the fort, as opposed to the bathroom. He has decided that his favorite flavor of glick—the local bug juice—is red (note that it's not called cherry glick, but, rather, simply red, appropriately representing its multiflavored composition).

Better yet, Pepe is gradually beginning to open up to his new family and comfortably adjust to being separated from his family back home. He's beginning to lose his anxiety about his mother back in Anaheim (all he talked about the first few days), and to settle into living on the shores of Lake Dunmore. He jokes and goofs frequently with his staffman Cameron MacDonald and the other three campers in his tent during rest hour. Twice a day for Indian Circle meeting, where announcements are made and activities started, he runs over to the *Waramaug* meeting area, sitting next to his favorite wigwam staffman or best friend of the day. While showing signs of feistiness, probably related to his small size, he's a happy camper.

At night, Aaron Lewis, the *Waramaug* director, points to the North Star. In Los Angeles, stars are masked by the lights and smog of the city, and Pepe is intrigued. Also, he's passionate about the camp food. While for years campers have typically bemoaned the culinary quality at Keewaydin, the bottomless dishes and humongous salad bar are a real treat for Pepe.

I wonder how aware Pepe is of the differences between him and most of the other campers. I wonder if the other *Waramaug* campers can tell that Pepe is not from a town like theirs, that Pepe thinks about survival and doesn't take it for granted. All the same, generations of young campers have gone through the same ups and downs their first few days. They've had the same bouts of insecurity as they fall asleep in their new cots for the first time.

Each day is new, each experience totally novel for Pepe. In many ways, that is true for all the kids here. The first of anything brings excitement, anticipation, and fear—fear of the unknown. Later this summer, it may be the fear of the known that some of the campers deal with; here, for Pepe, for now, it is the fear of the unknown.

A few days into the summer, in the early afternoon, as rest hour ends and *Waramaug* gathers at the Indian Circle, wigwam director Aaron Lewis addresses the kids. There are sixty-four campers in the wigwam during the first month's session, and then about half will leave and be replaced by new youngsters, keeping the roster about the same for both months. Of these sixty-four, Pepe might be the absolute smallest, not that this has slowed him down. He's tightly sandwiched in between two campers right now on a bench, feet dangling a good foot off the ground, sticklike arms crossed, listening attentively to Lewis, a middle school guidance counselor from Boston who took the time to show him the North Star a few nights ago.

"How many of you," Aaron Lewis is saying, "can tell me what Hare House is?"

A few campers raise their hands. Lewis picks on a redhead named Sam.

"It's the building next to Tent Four over there." He's pointing. "Well, it's not really a building. More like a room."

"That's right," replies Lewis. "And who can tell me what's in there?"

A few campers raise their hands again, and one is called. Pepe watches, not totally sure after his few days at camp where Hare House is, or what's inside it.

"There are a lot of pictures in there, and some books about Keewaydin and its history and stuff. And Waboos is in there a lot—it's sort of like his office."

"That's right," says Lewis. "Good. And you guys are welcome, whenever you want to, during free time, to go into Hare House, check it out, learn about the history of the camp, and ask Waboos questions. You're welcome—in fact, encouraged—to do that."

The Indian Circle then continues. After announcements like this are made, the activities for the afternoon are listed, and then the campers choose what they wish to do. Canoeing, swimming, soccer, and dramatics are among today's options.

Later, when the activity period ends around 4:30, making way for free time, a group of campers playing soccer

camp

end up near Tent 4, gabbing about the game and the duck that sits in a roped-off area around a nearby tree, nurturing several eggs that will soon hatch. Several feet away, the old man from the cottage is doing his slow-paced high-step walk back from his afternoon trip across the field. A few of the boys wander over to him as he approaches Hare House.

"Waboos, how many years have you been here?" one asks.

Kids—and adults, for that matter—will not typically show willing interest in such historical exploration. It's not that natural. You don't tell the average kid about an art museum down the block and expect to find him in the Impressionist exhibit the next afternoon. Somehow, Keewaydin is occupying a special place in these kids' hearts, and it leads them, without inhibition, to explore the institution's history, wanting to know more about their summer playground. The sense of tradition at the institution is that strong.

Waboos looks down at the camper who asked the question, somehow making eye contact despite not being able to make out the features of the boy's face. He smiles, the slits of his aged eyes closing tighter.

"Well, my first summer was back in 1923, but I missed a few years when I was in Europe taking care of that Hitler fellow, so not quite eighty years yet."

The boys nod, captivated by the oldest man they've ever seen, who was at their camp before their grandparents were born.

"Is Peter Hare related to you?" one of the boys asks.

"Yes, he runs the camp now, and he is my son" is the proud response.

"Wow . . . that's so cool. And where is your wife?" the boy asks, then pauses, suspecting even at his young age that he's ventured into difficult territory.

"Oh, she's not here this summer. She's not feeling well.

"Come on in, and I'll show you a picture of what Kee-waydin was like when I was a camper," he says, swiftly changing the subject. The boys wait for him to locate and negotiate the two steps into Hare House, then follow him inside.

chapter five

the freedom not to fail

present

Quenton "Q" Spratley is one cool kid.

It starts with his name, "Q." Everyone calls him that; it was even listed that way on the camper roster that was distributed to the *Waramaug* staffmen. Everyone remembers the camper with the letter for a name; it sets him apart from the pack immediately. Kids want to get to know him, and staffmen too—to find out what makes this camper so special that he's identified by a letter, while everyone else gets a name.

Q does not disappoint—he's a strikingly good-looking ten-year-old, the kind of kid who intrigues you by always seeming like he's got something else on his mind while you talk to him. Q's mother often wonders the same thing back home in Fullerton, when Q is reluctant to do his homework or his chores. The latter will get him punished; the homework so far has not been a problem, as Q is bright enough to make almost all *A*'s in his classes. Though in a living situation where money is tight and limited, Q has made success a big part of his young life, especially on the sports field. An incredibly adept athlete who picks up new sports easily, Q was discovered by Dave Wilk on the street outside his house in Fullerton, playing street hockey. Dave was recruiting for GOALS, trying to get more kids into his ice hockey program and off the streets. Within a few weeks of taking him to the rink and teaching him how to ice-skate, Q had become one of the standout players on his new team.

And so it is that during an early July day in Keewaydin's ninety-second year of operation, Q Spratley is one of the last boys to roll out of his cot on the banks of Lake Dunmore. Q is spending the month in Tent 7, which is three tents down from Pepe Molina's. The hockey skills Q has are a natural outgrowth of his athletic ability, which has been on full display so far at camp. While basketball is his best sport, he's also shown himself to be an excellent baseball player, boxer, swimmer, and diver.

Barely a week into the summer, Q has given up on his laundry and has comfortably settled into a one-outfit rotation consisting of black sweatpants, Adidas shower sandals, and a white tank-top undershirt that picks up a minor stain every day or so. On this morning, Q trudges across *Waramaug* ball field to the dining hall, where the entire camp is filing in for breakfast. The dining hall is one of many living relics of Keewaydin, built in the 1920s and full of all kinds of plaques, framed letters, and keepsakes that were, in most cases, probably hung without much thought over the years, and left hanging there. Amid the memorabilia, a few elements are striking: scores of banners and pennants from colleges and universities—my alma mater, Denison University, is somewhere up there—and flags of dozens of nations hanging from the ceiling, brought by campers from these countries. Also, by the main entrance onto the porch are two large and grand portraits, one of Waboos, which he probably sat for about five years ago, and next to that another that reads "Sid Negus, Keewaydin Director, 1926–1939."

Q and the rest of the camp, under a canoe hanging from the rafters, wolf down bowls of cereal and then some camp-edible French toast before filing out onto the field for morning formation (flag raising), and then back to their tents and cabins for cleanup and inspection. Thus, the day starts.

Peter Hare is, like many camp directors, at once invisible and ubiquitous. On one hand, you rarely know where he is any given moment, but, conversely, he seems to show up at any locale at any given time of the day. This morning, in the shadows of breakfast and formation, when the camp gathers for a cannon blast to start the day, Peter is conducting a daily meeting of his wigwam directors, outlining plans for the day. Meanwhile, campers make beds, sweep tent floors, and excavate missing socks, oblivious to the meeting and planning that goes on around them each morning.

Peter is what any parent hopes a camp director will be. His face is defined by what is best characterized as a permanent look of caring and concern—someone who is concerned about why your son might be unhappy, and who wants to know what would make him happy. While his older sister, Laurie, bears a close resemblance to their father, Waboos, with large round eyes and a long face, Peter looks more like his mother, with a smaller chin.

Peter Hare lives about fifteen minutes from camp, in a modern suburban development in Middlebury, but, like his father, his home is at camp. Peter grew up here, spending every summer of his young life at Keewaydin, first as a tot wandering around camp, then as a young camper, later as a staffman in *Wiantinaug*, and eventually, as the director of the whole *Wiantinaug* wigwam. Meanwhile, outside of camp, he was a formidable athlete, one who would eventually run track at Ohio Wesleyan. After college, Pete returned to school to teach Spanish, eventually becoming a department chair at Episcopal Academy near Philadelphia. Although he took a break from Keewaydin, spending some time abroad to explore his interest in Spanish cultures, he couldn't pass up the opportunity when the camp came calling for a new director a few years ago. He couldn't give up the chance to succeed his father, and to return to and lead the institution that, in many ways, had reared him.

As the new leader of Keewaydin—a veteran of over thirty summers here—Peter epitomizes the camp's succession plan. Peter will go over to his father in the dining hall, or during an activity, whisper something in his ear, share a joke. It makes you wonder if Waboos's confidence about walking around camp without being able to see is because he knows Peter—and his daughter, Laurie, who comes each summer from her home in Seattle to run the arts and crafts program, and his son Steve, who runs a health club year-round in Middlebury—are never far from him. I listen to Peter reflect upon Keewaydin, and I can hear his father's voice.

"Sid Negus used to use the term *planned freedom* to describe the day at Keewaydin," Waboos has told me more than once. "Planned freedom."

Waboos seems to have great fondness for Negus, the director in the 1920s and 1930s, as a boss and as a mentor. I only know him from his portrait in the dining hall, and maybe from a few stories my father told me. As Waboos tells it, each June, at the beginning of the summer, Sid would address the staff in the dining hall.

"Now, as the summer starts, remember two things," he'd say. "First, we've never had a serious accident at Keewaydin. So let's put it off for one more year."

A few staffmen would surely chuckle as Sid, who had a PhD in chemistry and spent winters as a distinguished college professor down south, punctuated the remark with a wink.

"And second, while maybe some camper doesn't look like much to you, try to remember that to some parent, he's worth a million dollars."

Here's what Sid Negus's idea of planned freedom means: During both morning and afternoon activity periods, campers at Keewaydin are given a wide selection of programs from which to choose. The activity periods are each followed by free time, to give the camper further freedom to do whatever he wants—work on his canoeing, play more basketball, or just hang out by the tents, playing cards and fooling around. It's pretty low-key, but at the same time, as Peter Hare notes, there is a plan.

"The coup system encourages kids to try new things and have a well-rounded summer," he tells me. "And we think that's a really crucial thing."

The coup system is essentially an offering of credit for participation in and mastery of activities at Keewaydin. It's been around since the days of Sid Negus, and coup boards—big wooden plaques with records of camper coups—are all over the camp. Campers earn coups by completing requirements in a variety of skills and activities. The more you do, the more you learn, the more you earn. The slanted ceiling of the dining hall and other cottages and cabins around camp serves as a record book of Keewaydin, dating back eighty years. I always look for my name, my father's name, and my sons' names on those boards; they are a biography of us all at camp, an everlasting testament to the challenges we met.

At a daily meeting before the day's afternoon activity period, *Waramaug* wigwam director Aaron Lewis reads off the list of options. In a wigwam of sixty-four campers, ten of whom are out on their canoe trips, there are about seven or eight activities to choose from, including a featured activity like baseball or soccer, which will attract upward of fifteen kids. The remainder of the activities will be small-group instruction—only three or four kids will do canoeing, and maybe even just one or two will choose to play tennis. The result is the opportunity for quick learning and mastery of new skills. Q in particular is a telling example of this: While he could have stuck with basketball and other familiar pursuits, he's frequently spotted at the diving dock, out fifty feet in Lake Dunmore, or in a kayak on the lake's shores.

Yet he's never tried mountain climbing, certainly not while living in Los Angeles; up until this summer, Q, like Pepe, has had little interaction with the backwoods of nature. Something, though, about the staffman's description of climbing, a new activity this summer, intrigues Q today, and he raises his hand to participate. I always hated hiking as a camper. To me it wasn't a sport. It was walking uphill. Who likes walking uphill? It took me another forty years and major heart surgery to understand the exercise value and aesthetic virtue of climbing a mountain.

Later in the evening, after Q and the campers go to sleep, Dan, the staffman in charge of mountain climbing, visits the dining hall, where off-duty staffers gather to socialize each night. Some sit at a table playing cards, others work on preparing for upcoming trips, and others flirt with some visiting staffers from Songadeewin (the likes of which, quite regrettably, weren't there when I was a staffer—the sister camp having reopened across the lake only a few years ago). While all this goes on, Dan brags in amazement to anyone who will listen about this kid named Q in *Waramaug* who climbed for the first time today, and, he swears, picked up the sport quicker than anyone he's ever seen, displaying nothing short of professional potential.

Keewaydin's planned freedom program is what encourages a kid like Q—who's already found a way to succeed in his young life with basketball and hockey—to expand his horizons and venture into other activities. For other kids, not as talented as Q, camp offers choices that may be easier than the winter options represented by school.

Many schools don't take into account that children are mentally structured in countless different ways and thus learn differently. Not only does a timed exam not test the full potential of every child, but school can fail to point every child in the direction of his or her abilities. Many more children could succeed if every teacher understood how the differently wired child learns. (I heartily recommend Dr. Mel Levine's book, *A Mind At a Time,* for a more comprehensive look at this issue.)

Camp can be a very reinforcing experience. Peter Hare puts it well: "You've never kayaked before, and you can learn how to roll a kayak," he says. "And you've never canoed before, and you learn how to paddle in the stern and keep that boat straight. These are challenges that help kids feel better about themselves, grow self-confident, build self-esteem. It's the idea of breaking a kid out of his comfort zone, and using new challenges as building blocks."

The next day, Pepe Molina sits quietly at the morning's Indian Circle. He's getting into the rhythm of Keewaydin, wearing his camp T-shirt with pride—it bears the Keewaydin triangular oars logo. But that he's wearing the shirt also bears a bit of ignominy; it's a shirt sold in the camp store for small children, not eleven-year-olds. Certainly other campers have noticed that Pepe is wearing a shirt that would fit their younger brothers and sisters.

Pepe seems to overcompensate for his diminutive stature with a brash and bold attitude toward his peers. No one wants to mess with Pepe—he'll talk back and let you hear it. This combative attitude transfers well to the sports field, where he is one of the more animated competitors in soccer and basketball. While he has clearly worked hard at his skills in these sports, his size is harder to overcome in athletic activities new to him. Unlike Q, Pepe is not a natural at anything he picks up.

For Pepe, the featured activity for the wigwam this morning is unattractive—ultimate Frisbee, a game he's never played. (The staffmen claim this—and juggling as well—are sports, but I won't acknowledge that until I see it on ESPN, and ESPN does broadcast everything from Ping-Pong to poker to the National Spelling Bee.)

Two enthusiastic staffmen—Benji and Graham—are running the activity. Pepe is persuaded to join and heads to *Waramaug* ball field with eleven other boys. The first few minutes are spent going over the rules and practicing how to throw a Frisbee—something else that's new to Pepe— and then the game begins. (For us novices like Pepe out there, ultimate Frisbee is something of an outdoor hybrid between basketball and football, in that the team has to pass the disklike Frisbee into an end zone for a score.) As expected, Pepe is not nearly as good at tossing the disk as several of the other boys, who have played the game for years.

Along the way, though, a funny thing happens. Benji, picking up on Pepe's tenacity and toughness, encourages him to channel that energy into defense. Sure enough, Pepe gets in the way of a few intended passes and becomes a point guard of his team's attack, starting several fast breaks with great plays. By the end of the game, he's worn out, but it's a good worn out, and he gets a few pats on the back for his effort, most notably from the staffmen.

Pepe is certainly receptive to the compliments, but he isn't so sure he wants to deal with this strange game again. Behind his tent, a game of basketball picks up, and he finds himself, as usual, joining in, back to his old self, hogging the ball as soon as his sneakers hit the dirt court.

Is it possible to fail summer camp? In the end, there are no sure things, and, yes, even at camp, some campers don't seem to blossom.

Sitting in Hare House, about a hundred feet from where Pepe is charging down the court, Waboos provides answers to my barrage of questions.

"Mike, you can't fail summer camp," he says in his trademark matter-of-fact way. It's a motto that he says he first coined some years back when another former camper, Alex Wolff, returned to camp to write an article about Keewaydin for *Sports Illustrated*. In the article, Wolff recalls one summer, when he struck out with the bases loaded in the bottom of the last inning. Disaster did not ensue—ten minutes later, Wolff recalls, he was happily shooting baskets on the nearby dirt court.

Waboos reasons that you can't fail summer camp, because if one challenge isn't kind to you, there's always another one waiting around the corner. The abundance of free time allows you to find what you want. Challenges are in abundance at camp, but so is freedom: freedom to play basketball every day, freedom to jump in the lake and splash water, freedom to just hang out. Freedom, in essence, from failure—or, more specifically, from having to ponder and reflect upon failure in its aftermath.

"I've figured out that all kids are really okay. You just have to get the right situation for them, and I figure camp can do a lot of good for guys who are not doing so well at home," Waboos says.

The Keewaydin philosophy is right for Keewaydin. The adult world, the workplace, the family environment—all are different from camp. But bringing some of camp's choices to our life still could be a goal, a model for us. My father didn't fail life, but his father and grandfather expected him to go to an Ivy League college (which he did), become a lawyer (which he did)—expected, expected, expected. He hated being a lawyer; he would have much preferred to have been an architect. And he would have been great, but family pressure and financial pressure set him in a different direction. If he had taken—or had been able to take—what he really learned at Keewaydin out into the world, he probably would have become an architect. I was lucky: He encouraged me to follow the Keewaydin way, or I might have become a doctor. I wrote plays in college because I (mistakenly) thought I could, and because I realized that I hated organic chemistry (and, in truth, grew less and less crazy about the sight of blood). I dropped the idea of medical school after graduating from college. Still experimenting, I tried something I learned at camp, being part of an organization, a team, even if it happened to be inserting the TV commercials into CBS's children's programs.

While certainly as a parent, the educational theories behind Keewaydin are interesting, here's what's really striking to me: The foundations of this quality of the camp go back decades. Today, they seem increasingly obvious as more and more educators realize that we are all wired differently and learn differently. The old director, Sid Negus, knew this eighty years ago, and now, thanks to his wisdom, Pepe and Q—in their own ways—are succeeding.

Then again, maybe I'm getting ahead of myself. It's only early July. They haven't even gone on their overnight canoe trips. And it is tripping, the teamwork, the risks from the elements, and the close association with nature, that really tests and develops a child. From the streets of California to the wilderness of Vermont—who knows what can happen?

chapter six

on the algonquin

1956

Three weeks in the wilderness.

Three weeks in the wilderness, with no prospect of seeing, hearing, or talking to anyone other than seven other campers and two staffmen. Three weeks in the wilderness carrying food in "wanagans" (large crates), pitching tents, paddling on and on through seemingly unending lakes in Canada's Algonquin Park. Carrying canoes over three-mile portages. The senior wilderness trip . . .

Only two days were left, two days before I would climb onto a truck with seven older boys (nine months older, at least), towing five canoes, hundreds of pounds of supplies, and shovels, tents, tarps, dehydrated food, and first-aid kits, transporting all this equipment twelve hours from Vermont to Canada. Two days to go, and now I was crippled with apprehension and stomachaches and dizziness. I could only think just one thing: How do I get out of it?

I'd gone on many trips at Keewaydin. I knew what it was to be exhausted. I had been lost in the Green Mountains. I had been stranded on the wrong side of a raging river after a rain. I had broken a paddle and scraped the bottom of a canoe. But I never had been in the woods for three straight weeks, and never been old enough to be (almost) responsible. And thus I was trying to figure how to get out of all this. Maybe I could fake getting sick (I really did feel sick). I sat by the lake, quietly trying to hide these feelings, plotting a phone call to suggest to my parents that . . . I couldn't think what to suggest.

I was fourteen years old, preparing to go on the most cherished trip the camp had to offer. I had begged and pleaded to go on the trip. I could think of no higher honor, no greater status than to be among the select few who would be picked. Then I was picked.

And I became petrified. I had nobody to confide in because all the other boys were obviously excited, cheerily packing the food, the canoe paddles, their duffel bags, and their gear. I was silent. I was scared. I was in a fog, and instead of helping to fill out the daily meal schedule and supply the first-aid kits, I sat around, useless. No, I didn't get homesick; that was for the little kids. But I was trapped, and the more trapped I felt, the more panicked I got.

I tried to keep reminding myself of the challenging hikes I had taken without a second thought, the long paddles against headwinds stoking feelings of exhaustion and exhilaration, not fear. There, without complaining, I had done the duties of other campers who came down sick. I had chopped wood without cutting off my leg, and I had bushwhacked through dense trees, looking for a discreet place not to have my rear bitten off by mosquitoes. I had learned the language of the canoe, to pole up a river, to carry it like a tray of glass, to protect it, to breathe in its capsized air pocket. All of that was second nature until now . . . sitting on the lake, my mind racing—racing, and focusing on nothing.

The eight boys would be divided into four teams for this trip. At each campsite, one team would pitch the tents, one would build the campfire, one would cook the meal, and one would "wallop," meaning wash the dishes. The next day, responsibilities would rotate. My partner, Baird Morgan, was ideal. He was the strongest, oldest, and best stern canoe man in the camp. (A canoe, like any boat, has a front and a rear—a bow and a stern. The person in the stern steers and leads the boat.) Now, before the trip began, he and I, as a team, were supposed to do our share during the on-campus preparation for the trip. We were assigned to patch the tents. It's hard to patch tents when you're completely unfocused. And without the tents— tents that dated back to World War II and, in some cases, World War I—patched up, rain would cause puddles or even little ponds where there was supposed to be dry shelter. A sleeping bag is the most important piece of equipment on a trip. Once it gets wet, there's no escaping the hostility of nature. Wet clothes or a wet sleeping bag are the devil's work on a wilderness canoe trip.

Brownie, our trip leader, was a staffman, and he seemed at least a hundred years old in my mind, although he was actually forty. He had a strange hole behind his ear (almost like a bullet hole), which I was afraid to examine closely. He came over to me and sat down.

"You know," he began, "I'm always nervous before these big trips."

It took everything in my power not to look over at that hole, as I visualized its outline in my brain.

"Sometimes I get afraid of things that I build up in my mind," he said.

I turned and looked at him as he continued.

"I sometimes think things are more dangerous than they really are, but then I calm myself down and work through the problem and realize that I'm safe and I'll have a good time. I always end up laughing at myself and wonder why I got afraid in the first place."

"Yeah," I responded.

"Funny, isn't it?" he said, and got up and walked away.

We left for Canada two days later. The trip up in the back of the army surplus truck was windy, the atmosphere festive. I usually found "100 Bottles of Beer on the Wall" to be a catchy tune, but this time I didn't sing. On the way up, the sightseeing in Quebec City was cool, though I remained withdrawn from the group. By the time we finally reached the wilderness, I had a nagging case of internal butterflies. They were butterflies I recognized from my first day of school, butterflies I remembered from putting a first toe in the water at Jones Beach on Long Island, butterflies

I recalled from jumping a horse over fences, following my reckless father down a rocky path.

Once we got going, though, the butterflies vanished. Brownie's reassurance had helped. I didn't know exactly why, but slowly I could talk again and do the things I had done on previous trips. And on the first day, I even survived after capsizing while going over a waterfall—a small waterfall, but a waterfall nonetheless. A little later, I felt exhilaration as the daunting novelty of shooting rapids and creating campsites, with no parents or siblings in sight, became a nonstop adventure of self-reliance, of teamwork . . . and, yes, even of leadership. The only time I sat alone again by the lake was to brush my teeth. Portaging—carrying the canoes over land—became the challenge at hand, eight boys walking along the railroad ties, contesting who could carry the most in the quickest time. My anger directed at whoever spaced those railroad ties continues to this day. They are too close together to step on each one, and too far apart to step on every other one. And, of course, the rail was too thin to walk on except for future Cirque de Soleil performers. Instead, on these portages, the ties were ripe for tripping, and for learning new expletives.

Long days paddling became the time to write the trip song. Shooting rapids provided the roller-coaster adventures of the trip. Finding great campsites, collecting wood, cooking morning bread, telling stories, living off the land, and eating prepacked dried food or peanut butter were the rewards.

We arrived back at our camp in Vermont to a heroes' welcome from 150 more junior campers. As we put away the tarps from the trip, Brownie came up to me.

"Mike, we had a great trip, don't you think?" he asked. "It's great you were on the team." He smiled in a way that I knew he knew. He smiled in a way that I knew he wouldn't tell anybody what he knew. He smiled in a way that has connected him to my life forever, though I would rarely ever see him again.

I now tried to look into that little hole in his head to see if I could fathom what was inside. I looked, and gleaned my last lesson of the trip: Wisdom can't be seen.

Funny, isn't it?

chapter seven

help the other fellow

present

I stand next to Waboos, looking at a wooden board hanging on the wall, one that I must have looked at a thousand times over the years. We've wandered into Keewaydin's dining hall, a huge room that alternates between smelling like the food that's eaten there and smelling like the solvents that are used to clean it.

What's currently attracting my attention, though, is not the smell of the air, or the hundreds of other items crammed on the walls—school pennants posted by campers, flags, coup boards, "older-timer" boards, fading paddles, and antlers nailed up years before. Instead, I'm focused on a plaque on the wall in front of me, above the piano on the stage platform. The plaque is roughly the size of a movie poster, with words neatly printed in white paint on a black background, like a permanently marked-on chalkboard.

The top of the plaque reads: AN IDEAL CAMPER MUST . . . Beneath this are a series of completed phrases that indicate what in fact an ideal camper must do: AN IDEAL CAMPER MUST BE HONEST AND LOYAL. BE MODEST. ALWAYS BE WILLING TO HELP. AVOID CRABBING. BE A LEADER. BE BROAD-MINDED. TAKE HIS MEDICINE WHEN HE DESERVES IT. There are fourteen of these in all. I read down the list of the mantras, the instructions for the camper who strives to be ideal. I reach the bottom: BE WILLING TO HELP THE OTHER FELLOW.

On a campus filled with sayings, slogans, and mottoes, the single maxim at Keewaydin that is most often heard is "Help the other fellow." Apparently, this particular dictum dates all the way back to the days of Commodore Clarke. It's posted on signs at camp, and is oft repeated by staffmen in formal settings (the Sunday service) and at informal gatherings (for example, inspection, where a staffman may ask a camper to "help the other fellow" and pick up some-one else's tennis racket or comic book off the floor).

It's a simple saying, and certainly a virtuous one, but also one that, understandably, might feel a bit stilted today. Yes, to "help the other fellow" is to do the "right thing," but so what? There needs to be some impetus, some reason, some cause-and-effect relationship that drives young campers to act in such a way. That's why tripping is so central to Kee-waydin's core values.

Pepe Molina is probably as nervous as I was before my senior wilderness trip. He finds himself part of a group about to head westward in a canoe on Lake George. Tripping is as old as any tradition at Keewaydin; in fact, it's the reason the camp exists at all. Commodore Clarke founded the original Keewaydin Temagami in Canada solely as a tripping camp. When parents of twelve- and thirteen-year-old boys convinced Clarke to open a camp a little closer to civilization, in Salisbury, Vermont, the tripping heritage remained. Every wigwam gets involved, from the one-night *Annwi* trips to *Moosalamoo*'s three-week tour of the Verendrye in Canada. Pepe's group left this morning from camp, headed for Lake George, as part of the second batch of *Waramaug* campers to depart, just a few days after Q's group headed to Little Tupper Lake and what's called the Whitney Wilderness area in the Adirondack Forest Preserve.

Evan and James, the staff leaders on Pepe's trip, are already a bit on edge; a few of the eight campers, including Pepe, have proven themselves to be somewhat volatile during their first few weeks at camp. It's Evan's first time leading a trip; he went on several during his days at camp, though, and knows the intensity of the experience, especially for young *Waramaug* campers. While the campers on these trips assume some of the burden with regard to paddling canoes, pitching tents, and cooking meals, it's up to the staffmen to make up for what the ten- and eleven-year-olds can't do. The staff must also be attentive to inklings of possible crisis—ranging from childish squabbling among the trippers to more serious safety issues in the woods.

During the "shakedown," or predeparture discussion before Pepe's trip, the campers engaged in several arguments,

and while "packing out," or preparing all the food and supplies for the trip, an actual fight broke out. Pepe wasn't directly involved, but he could have been. His size, combined
with a take-no-prisoners attitude, seems to invite conflict,
especially in a situation like this, where the kids are scared
and anxious about the trip, not that they'd admit it. Fortunately, the van ride this morning has been calming—the
campers are entranced by the sudden change in scenery
from the confines of Keewaydin, where they've been isolated for nearly two weeks. When I went to Lake George
as a *Waramaug* camper, you could drink right out of the
water. Nowadays, with the lake much more populated,
that's no longer permitted. But on a sunny summer day, it's
still a sight to behold.

On the shore, after the van departs, Pepe and seven others gingerly step into four canoes, supplies and equipment
in tow. The canoes with a staffman and camper carry a lot
of the supplies; the wanagan supply boxes, tents, and water
jugs are placed in the bow of the boat with the camper to
maintain weight balance. Each camper canoe carries the
two kids' duffel bags in them and other necessities. While
out on the water, with just two to a boat, the campers—
for the moment—seem to be getting along. Pepe and the
others have quieted down since climbing into the water,
and the rhythm of the five canoes smoothly floating in the
lake is the calming rhythm that dominates the trip right
now.

Q Spratley and trip leader Michael Sotir are 150 miles away from Pepe's trip, amid the islands of Little Tupper Lake. Unlike Lake George, the Whitney Wilderness is protected from population, maintaining its remote environment. Even the park rangers paddle from one location to another in canoes—no motorboats allowed. During the shakedown, Michael Sotir observed that nobody on the trip—camper or staffman—had been on this trip before, thus making it a true exploratory adventure. A ranger who briefed them noted that the area has a significant black bear population. Sure enough, no more than ten feet from the parking lot, the group came upon a pile of black bear scat, or dung. From there, a certain new sense of danger took over. When later that night Michael gave the trippers the option of staying on the mainland or on one of the many small islands that dot the shoreline of the lake, Q did not disagree with the unanimous consensus to stay on an island, a long swim away for any bears.

Michael Sotir is one of a handful of staffmen in *Waramaug* beyond college years; in fact, he has two sons in the wigwam himself. A house builder in Baltimore, Michael, along with his wife, Carolyn, a songwriter and television producer, decided to spend a few weeks at Keewaydin with their children a couple years back. That's all it took—they were hooked, and Michael decided to get all his construction projects done by mid-June, take summers off, and become a staffman at Keewaydin while his sons were campers there. Carolyn is now one of several women who live and work at Keewaydin, singing a good-night song to *Wara-*

maug each night, helping out with barbecues and special events.

Concerned about Q's lack of experience, Michael decides to make Q his bowman. This is a propitious decision, because Q, continuing his pattern of picking up physical activities quickly, has proven himself to be one of the best canoemen on the trip. During their days on the water, Q and Michael have gotten a chance to talk, and the contractor from suburban Baltimore has been quite impressed with the youngster from the streets of Fullerton. While Q is a reserved kid, he's clearly bright, and, Michael notices, used to responsibility, being the oldest kid in a household with a working mother.

On the last day of their trip, Q asks Michael about an island a short distance away. When no one else wants to go, the two of them decide to swim out to the island to check it out for themselves. They relax on the island for a few minutes, when suddenly there is a rustling in the woods behind them.

"Do you think there are any black bears who might be able to swim out here and hang out?" asks Q.

Michael ponders the question for a moment and glances anxiously into the woods behind him.

"I doubt it, but anything is possible."

More rustling.

"Let's swim back and see what the rest of the group is doing," Q suggests.

Keewaydin director Peter Hare has an interesting perception of the role of tripping in the camp framework. He says that while the activities within the camp foster independence among campers, the tripping fosters interdependence.

"When you go on a trip," he says, "everybody has a role and everybody has to chip in, and you're all depending on one another. It's not like at home, when you can close yourself off in your own room."

While the concept of this division of labor could be taught and exemplified anywhere—in a factory, on a sports team, in a group project at school—what separates the tripping experience is the stakes. Eight boys in the wilderness, each doing his own thing, doesn't work. Everyone must do their jobs at the campsite for the sake of the team. If there is any problem, like a loss of supplies or food, the group has to find a way to solve the dilemma. If, while sleeping in tents on an island, a camper or staffman wakes up to the sounds of black bears (it's unlikely, but not impossible) rustling through the trash, there's no time-out button that can be suddenly activated to defuse danger.

Some uncertainty, though, leads to impassioned team spirit. On a trip, no one is making fun of the kid who can't light a fire or pitch a tent; they're showing him how to do it and encouraging any progress. Necessity leads to team spirit; adventure leads to friendship. If a camper seems uneasy about portaging, and you're his partner in the canoe, it's best to offer encouragement (tell him he's strong enough) before your canoe—and you—are facedown in the mud. And some reasonable fear of the unknown leads to maturity and toughness. Each camper is compelled to grow up instantly, becoming a youngster who pitches the best tent and paddles the strongest canoe. Keeping a canoe on a straight course becomes very important all of a sudden. Here is where you test what you learned back in camp about the K stroke, the little twist of the body that keeps you in a straight line.

Ultimately, what these challenges lead to is a new and triumphant sense of achievement. While it's great to hit a home run or get the best score on some school exam, it's a much deeper and more satisfying success to win—to survive—as a team. Because that new team, the team that leaves camp in a van as two staffmen and eight campers, returns as a single body, a group with a new bond, tied together by adversity in the wild, a trip song, inside jokes told around the campfire.

So then, "Help the other fellow" is not a piece of empty rhetoric on a plaque at Keewaydin. Instead, it's an authentic way of life that begins on the trip, where it all makes sense.

Unfortunately, a few days later, on Lake George, there is no prevailing motto on Pepe Molina's *Waramaug* trip. Despite two productive days on the lake in canoes, tempers have once again flared up among the campers. Every time Evan and James think that they've put out one emotional fire, another one seems to crop up. Meanwhile, the wind that so conveniently helped move the canoes down the lake at the beginning of the trip has now become a violent headwind, and the staffmen have had to suspend canoeing and remain at their current campsite.

Squabbles continue. Several of the boys, including Pepe, go over to the water, playing among the pebbles and rocks as dusk begins to fall in. And oddly enough—maybe it's the placidity of the slowly setting sun and the sounds of the lake—the boys begin quietly chatting. After all the problems, they need to make it through one more night. The conversation somehow turns to parents and family. One camper talks about his parents and sister back home, and another talks about a divorced father who lives in another state. One kid says his father was once in jail, and another volunteers that his father should be in jail.

This is finally familiar territory for Pepe, who tells the group, no matter how odd it sounds coming from an eleven-year-old, how much he loves his mother, and how much she loves him, and how hard she works for him. He also talks of a father he doesn't know, in a city far away. After all the difficulty that the group has endured, the boys have worn themselves out from fighting and are finally bonding. They're no longer kids from Westchester and Connecticut and Orange County, California. They're members of the same trip.

The evening activity is a unique one: Using one of the tents, the campers make a sweat lodge—a saunalike atmosphere created by heating up stones in the fire and putting them inside the tent. The boys take turns sitting in the steaming tent for a few minutes, then jump into the lake to cool off. It's a highlight of the trip, as the stress of everything else is metaphorically sweated away and rinsed off.

The trip has taken a final turn. It's actually now an adventure to remember. "You had to be there" becomes the catch phrase for the trippers. You never return from a trip really able to recount and give the true flavor of the experience to someone who was not on the trip.

Most heartening about the whole story to me is a coda that Evan and James provide back at camp a few days later. Sitting on the lake's edge, waiting in a parking lot for the van to pick them up, Pepe proudly expresses how much he liked the trip. The fact that he was uncomfortable in the beginning, unhappy to be in the woods for five days, uncertain about teamwork—this is a silent memory of the past. Pepe proudly announces that he now believes they had the best team of any trip that summer. He was embracing the group, realizing what it means to be on a Keewaydin trip.

Years ago, a few days after we returned from the Algonquin trip, a letter from Keewaydin arrived at our family's house in Bedford Hills. It was from Brownie, the trip leader. Staffmen write letters home to parents during the summer to update them on their kids' progress at camp. It's not so much what it said—that I was one of the better trippers on the Algonquin—but, rather, what it meant, especially to my father. It was the Keewaydin way of saying that I had succeeded. I had met the ultimate challenge, and while I may have pleased, or at times displeased, my father in other ways, that letter showed him who I was, or who I could be.

In my business life, I've learned that the group is much better as a whole than any of the individuals separately. Working in business can be another canoe trip. It's about figuring out different roles for people, and those people fulfilling their tasks. It's about, as my friend John Angelo says, determining, in a pinch, who can sit in the stern of their canoe and set the course and who is better suited for the bow.

That said, subscribing to this virtue in the business world often meets resistance. How does one work in a team and "help the other fellow" when so much else is fueled by jealousy, envy, and greed? Do money and competitiveness create the environment to ignore, or even deceive the other fellow? Does entrepreneurship breed a general desire to unseat the other fellow, who is going after your idea, your promotion, or your job? These concerns are legitimate. Just as it is at Keewaydin, the challenge in business is to foster an enthusiastic atmosphere of teamwork that becomes self-reinforcing.

It's tough, though. The world is not camp—and that's too bad.

chapter eight

second place

1955

When John Angelo was growing up down the street from me with his single-parent mother, my father became his surrogate father. The friendship went back two generations; our grandparents knew one another, and our mothers were best friends. My father watched over John's family, and balanced his mother's checkbook. Meanwhile, John and I went to the same grade school, Allen Stevenson in New York. John's mother dated Mr. Waters, our English teacher. Later, we married roommates in New York City, and we are both still married to the same great women, Jane Breckenridge and Judy Hart.

In 1950, as soon as I got home from my first summer at Keewaydin, the first thing I did was tell John all about it. There was no doubt he was going to join me the following summer, and, accordingly, I decided at Christmas to drag him to the camp's winter reunion at the St. George Hotel in Manhattan. At the lunch, John and I sat down and said hello to everyone, then stood for the camp song. I sang along loudly to show off to John, who, of course, didn't know the song. I was a beat behind most of the way, as the song sounded different from the way I remembered it, but then again, we were in Manhattan, not Vermont, and everything seemed different. Then a prayer to start the meal; I said "Amen."

We started eating, and I felt a tap on the back. It was Waboos. Smiling, he led us from the table and walked out of the banquet room, down a hallway, and into another room, where the faces were more familiar.

I had gone to the wrong camp's reunion.

It was not an auspicious start to John's camp career. He still makes jokes about it at my expense, doesn't trust my sense of direction, and insists to this day on being the one who picks our meeting spots. But he did go to camp with me anyway in 1951 and the years that followed. My parents and John's mother always visited us together at mid-season. As I went to camp a year before John, I remained the expert in all things Keewaydin. Besides, John never cared for the bugs, the mud, the portaging, and all the things about the place that I loved. He had a good time, but, as he'd readily admit to you today, he would have preferred a baseball camp with the accommodations of a bed-and-breakfast to the tents that Keewaydin offered.

In 1955, I was thirteen years old, a camper in *Wiantinaug*, in Tent 10, at Keewaydin as usual for the full eight-week season. By the seventh week, I was riding the high of another great summer; I had already been on an Adirondack canoe trip, a Mount Mansfield hiking trip, and a five-day Saranac Lake trip. Furthermore, I had passed nearly all the requirements to get several coup certificates, given for completing requirements in a wide variety of activities. There were required coups to be won, like swimming and canoeing and tripping, plus elective coups from an assortment of activities that would give the camper the needed number for the certificate. Ninety-nine percent of these elective coups were drawn from rugged camping experiences, but the silliest among them—the dipping coup and the silence coup—had an appeal to me.

The dipping coup was given to campers who for a series of successive days jumped into the frigid water of Lake Dunmore at 7:00 A.M. for a dip. It was agony then, and surely it remains agony now. I don't think I ever made it to the lake more than three out of the thirty days at this early hour. That dip is like an 8:00 A.M. class at college. The mind has a yearning, but the body won't respond. Anyway, I eventually abandoned the dipping coup.

The silence coup was awarded to campers who managed to stay silent for an entire day. Once again, though this didn't exactly coincide with my real interests at camp, it was a challenge. I thought it should be a simple thing to do, not to speak for twenty-four hours. I tried several times during the early days of that summer, and several times I failed, at one point or another tricked by other campers into offering my opinion about something. Finally, with just a few days to go that summer, I managed to stay silent for most of an entire day, learning, unfortunately, that "close doesn't count." Perhaps it was why, on the way home that summer, I yelled and screamed with the rest of the kids on the bus all the way from Vermont to New York City. As a result, I lost my voice for two months. I couldn't talk until October. I didn't get a coup, and I've been hoarse for the fifty years since. At least it gives my hosting of our *Wonderful World of Disney* show a unique sound.

The final week of camp meant that the awards ceremony at the Indian Circle wasn't far away, and my attention, admittedly, was strongly focused in that direction. I was confident that I would win several awards that night. Within my grasp, I thought, was best tripper in *Wiantinaug*, and best canoeman, possibly best boxer, best sailor, and best tennis player, and maybe even best all-around camper. Tripping and canoeing were the most prestigious. The best canoeman in the entire camp, the winner of what was known as the Talmen Competition, was awarded the Eisner trophy. I knew I wouldn't win that one—it was almost always awarded to a camper from the oldest wigwam, *Moosalamoo*. I assumed everyone in camp believed that the award had been named for my family because my father or uncle— or both—had been such great canoemen.

That night, the senior staffman who stood in front of the camp assembly clarified the origin of the award. He noted, "We thank Mike Eisner's father for donating this trophy to the camp, a beautiful silver canoe made at Tiffany in New York." The award, it was suddenly clear to everyone, was named for my family because we had donated it (something I had never mentioned to anyone), not because we had mastered the treasured skill it honored. Omitting is the same as misleading. I felt embarrassed.

The fire in the center of the circle was glowing as 250 campers sat waiting to hear the winners' names called. Best tripper in *Wiantinaug* passed me by, as had best canoeman. I gulped.

Immediately after came best camper; they wouldn't wait for the end to announce this big honor; this wasn't the Academy Awards. I stared silently at the fire when my name wasn't announced for this prestigious trophy. Even though Keewaydin wasn't a competitive camp, I was still a competitive boy, and I quickly tried to determine by process of elimination what award could still be open to me. Some apprehension was setting in.

The boxing award, I soon realized, would be next. A week earlier had been the final boxing card of the year—kids from the different wigwams squaring off in front of the rest of the camp. And I was ready. Earlier in the summer, at midseason, I had suffered a regrettable experience in the boxing ring. My parents were there, and of course, so was John's mother. John and I were to square off against each other, best friend against best friend. We were in the ring, ready to fight, but within thirty seconds of starting, we got the giggles. It had been pretty embarrassing, and the fight was called. Our mothers were happy, I suspect, because we didn't get bloodied, but my father had seemed somewhat vexed. He didn't say anything. I perhaps got the message, and in my final boxing match, against a new foe, I won big-time.

When the ceremony got to the award, though, I came up short again. And my unhappiness grew. I thought I might have one more opportunity for an award, but after best sailor was given to someone else, all that remained to be announced was best tennis player. For the previous few weeks, I had worked my way through the wigwam tournament, then advanced to the final. But on the other side of the net was John. The final had taken place that very morning, the morning of the awards ceremony. It was a contest much anticipated, at least by us, fighting it out for best tennis player. I had beaten John the preceding two years in *Waramaug,* but in those two years I had grown a lot. My feet were too big for my body, and my body was too tall for my control. I wasn't as good an athlete, while John, conversely, had gotten better. I lost the match, and had conveniently also "lost" its details until this past New Year's Day, when I was coming out of a movie theater in Westwood, California, and decided to broach the question to John.

"Do you have any idea what the score was during the finals of the camp tennis tournament in 1955?" Without a beat, he replied, "I won, I believe, is the right answer! Third set, you were up 5–2, 40–15 and lost. You want to get coffee?"

"What? I was one point from winning? How do you remember that?" I asked.

"How could I forget that kind of comeback? I was finished. The fight had gone out of me, and I was completely prepared to finish second."

We walked across Westwood Boulevard. And he went on. "You served. I hit the ball to your backhand and raced to the net. Trying to end the match, you lobbed the ball over my head. It was long: 40–30, again—match point. You served. I repeated the strategy. This time you swung over the ball, and it sailed into the net. Deuce."

We entered Starbucks. He went on and on. "On the next serve I changed strategy. I hit to your forehand. You were protecting your backhand as you always did and you never moved. Then, uncharacteristically, you double-faulted. The match was mine."

"What kind of coffee do you want?"

"As the air left your body, I received an adrenaline charge so great that in that moment, I knew I was unbeatable. I won the next four games as well as the third set. The monkey was finally off my back. I finally beat you."

"One cappuccino, one regular coffee with milk, one espresso, and one frappuccino," I ordered. John was on a final fifty-year victory lap, amazing given that we hadn't once discussed this since the middle of the last century.

"The only piece of memorabilia on display in my dressing room," he said, "is a small bronze statue from that tournament. It's a young man with his serving arm broken off, much like a Roman statue. I look at it often. It never fails to make me smile. I had won Wimbledon and the U.S. Open all in one.

"Do you remember the match with Waboos and

Abby?" he asked as we walked back to the car. "Wasn't it that afternoon just before the awards ceremony?"

Later that afternoon at Keewaydin in 1955, after what appeared to be my big loss of the day, during free time before the awards ceremony, Waboos and Abby Fenn had finally agreed to play John and me in a doubles match, taking up a summer-long challenge we had issued them. We had been baiting them, pushing for a match—young, agile, and fast against old, slow, and just short of dyspeptic. The entire camp—or what seemed like it—had come out to see the match. But they played soft, with a Texas slice from Abby and continual drop shots from Waboos. They killed us—more humiliation!

No matter—that night at the Indian Circle, John got up to accept his award, clearly no longer upset about our exhibition loss to the directors. I stayed seated, like the majority of the other campers. All evening, I had stayed in my spot, never getting up in front of the whole camp to receive anything, except my coup certificate with thirty other boys. I must have come in second, I comforted myself, in sailing and boxing and tennis. I felt isolated as I walked back to my tent. It was soon bedtime, after brushing our teeth, taps, and the good-night song. I lay awake feeling something that even today is hard to describe—kind of like waiting after a job interview for a phone call that you know will never come.

The next morning, I woke up, and in my first few seconds of consciousness, I had those elusive feelings of "I know I'm upset at something, but I just can't quite remember." And then I remembered. I stumbled out of my cot to the fort, then came back and slipped on a pair of shorts and a relatively clean shirt for breakfast. I looked at the boys around me, saying nothing of my disappointment from the night before. I simply walked off to the dining hall.

On my way, there was suddenly someone next to me: the someone who had cost me my tennis award. John looked over at me, and I looked back.

"Are you packed?" he asked. We would be going home together later in the day.

"You're kidding," I answered abruptly.

"There's no inspection today. Let's play tennis after breakfast," he said.

For some reason, it seemed like a good idea. Maybe it was because I liked to play tennis, or maybe, frankly, I just liked the fact that I might be able to have another shot at beating him. For the record, I also asked John if he remembered who won this rematch. Graciously, since it's my book, he agreed to let me say I did.

Years later, admittedly, it's tough to reconcile my competitive urges with Keewaydin's "be a fair winner and a good loser" philosophy. The fact is, one remembers his losses more vividly than any successes because losing stings. Losing is solitary, while winning is crowded; everyone has room for a winner. The Keewaydin idea that you can't fail summer camp, that you can always start over again, that there'll always be another match with John Angelo, is something that stays with you forever. And you never forget a comeback.

chapter nine

a fair winner and good loser

present

On a well-swept dirt court, the bounce of a basketball is truer than you might think. Sure, rocks, pebbles, and the occasional twig make for a bit of a Boston Garden–like unpredictability, but for the most part, the ball comes back to your hand pretty much where you think it should. This fact is largely irrelevant to the ten- and eleven-year-olds currently playing basketball on the dirt court in *Waramaug.* (In 2003 the camp built a concrete court near the laundry barn after ninety years of dirt. For those of us against any change at Keewaydin, this was acceptable.)

For nine of the boys, this fact is irrelevant because they haven't yet mastered the art of dribbling a basketball without looking down to see what they are doing. They will probably learn this skill in a year or so, but for now, ball goes down means head goes down. For the tenth boy, however, the exact trajectory of the bounce of the ball is, in fact, a relevant element to his game. Not only can he easily dribble downcourt while keeping his head cocked straight ahead, but he has also been known to let the ball barely bounce while speedily dribbling to the basket. He's just as likely to let it bounce masterfully off the front of his bent knee and back to the ground once or twice—essentially dribbling with his legs—before returning the ball to the normal bouncing pattern of hand to ground and back to hand. It's a Globetrotter-like move, the likes of which have probably never been seen on the *Waramaug* court.

And when Q Spratley successfully pulls off his knee-dribbling move en route to a killer crossover basket past a bewildered defender, the rest of the kids in the game shake their heads, and any staffman watching shakes his head as well.

Another kind of reaction, not as dazzling perhaps, but in some ways just as neat to watch, is prompted when another camper in the game, a boy under four feet and no heavier than fifty pounds, finally gets the ball. Each time up and down the court, he screams for it—"I'm open, I'm OPEN! Hey, here! Hey, HERE! Yo yo yo YO!"—desperately pleading with skeptical teammates to share the ball with him. He could be trailing a fast break with his four teammates up ahead, all undefended, and he'd still be calling for the ball.

When he does get it, the same thing tends to happen time and again. He sets his feet, wherever he is—usually no farther than ten or twelve feet from the basket—and uncorks a one-and-a-half-handed jump shot, in a style akin to an adult shot-putting a bowling ball. And more often than not, the ball rattles through the net. With each of these successful shots, Pepe Molina's confidence grows.

camp

It's a beautiful day at Keewaydin, and the sun is shining down on the *Waramaug* dirt court during morning free time, the very same court where I played, with the same glare, making it a bit tough to shoot from the left side on the far basket. Q has just penetrated through the lane, dribbling behind his back, nearly losing the ball, then getting it back and laying it in underhand. A few minutes before, Pepe—today, they happen to be playing on the same team—sank his third basket of the game, a moon-shot jumper from out near where the free-throw line would be if the court were painted.

These are happy moments for Q and Pepe, and if you asked them what their favorite activities are at camp, basketball would certainly be at the top of the list. Yet if you look a little more closely at the game, you might see some potential problems.

You'll see Q, the star player in the game, show little patience for the kids on his team who aren't blessed with his skills. He hogs the ball, and on one or two occasions, he even steals the ball from them—his own teammates!—when they're not looking.

You'll hear Pepe's nonstop soprano chatter and realize that his irresistible smile belies some pretty heavy-duty trash talking for an eleven-year-old. Another boy encourages him to pass more; Pepe criticizes the boy's lack of shooting ability with a snicker. Another camper plays some tough defense on him, stealing the ball; Pepe fakes a fall onto the dirt, claiming a foul where there was none.

In truth, some observers might applaud the behavior of the two boys; after all, they're really just doing everything they can to win. If they were playing in a high school game, their coach might even instruct them to be doing some of the things they're doing—foul if you can get away with it, intimidate the other team—to give their team a better chance to win.

At Keewaydin, it's never been about winning and losing. It's about something more.

Sports have long been part of Keewaydin and Keewaydin culture. There's also something of an athletic legacy that Keewaydin campers have created throughout the years. Dick Harter, a longtime assistant coach in the NBA, was a Keewaydin camper in the 1940s, the son of Doc Harter, the camp doctor before Dr. McPhee, John McPhee's father. Jim Fullerton, head of *Moosalamoo* in my day, was the hockey coach at Brown. Also, as I mentioned earlier, Alex Wolff, the *Sports Illustrated* writer and author of *Big Game, Small World,* a smart book about the globalization of basketball, also spent his summers on the dirt court shooting baskets. Scores of other Keewaydin campers have gone on to big-time college play.

That said, while sports compose a pretty significant chunk of Keewaydin life, the camp is by no means a *sports camp.* Where else but at Keewaydin could I be head of tennis instruction? I was a decent player, but certainly not a great one at sixteen, and definitely without teaching credentials.

Returning to Keewaydin this summer, a few things strike me about the value of sports at Keewaydin. Sports help campers make friends. As much as tripping forges close bonds between campers and staffmen, initial friendship making at the beginning of camp often takes place on the basketball court or the soccer field. In addition, thanks to Keewaydin's small size, everyone can play the sports they want at camp without spending much time on the bench (as they might at school).

Of course, along with these potential benefits, there are also risks, risks on display on the *Waramaug* basketball court. Although Q and Pepe's team won, not all the campers left the court feeling too great about the pickup game. Toward the end, Pepe's trash talking escalated to a confrontation, in which a much larger kid pegged the ball at Pepe's feet. Leaving for lunch after the gong sounded, a few other kids seemed to walk off dejected; maybe they didn't get the ball enough, or perhaps were upset by the tone of the game.

The featured afternoon activity today is a baseball game on *Waramaug* ball field. The Nasty North, Pepe's team, is pitted against the Wild West, Q's team. Each team has about fifteen campers, who will rotate positions in the field, including that of pitcher. By the end of the third inning, the North has a huge lead, the score now eleven to four. Pepe, not as skilled in baseball as he is in basketball and hockey, has struck out on his trip to the plate, as Q has done, after hitting two sharp foul balls that came within a few feet of being extra-base hits.

Staffman Al Black umpires the game and lays out the rules for the campers before the first pitch: no arguing with the umpire; no walking on and off the field (you have to hustle out to your position); and no booing. Cheer on your teammates as much as you'd like, but don't boo or taunt the other team.

In the fifth inning, a camper named Sam, one of Pepe's tent mates and also one of the few kids in *Waramaug* almost as small as Pepe, steps to the plate. Sam is an American but lives in South Africa; thus, he has not played much baseball except during his summers at Keewaydin. Staffmen have taken time during free time to pitch to him and work on his techniques, and little by little, he's starting to show some improvement.

And now, as he steps to the plate, with his team losing by nine runs and the game ostensibly out of reach, his teammates creep closer to the third-base line to start cheering him on, with Pepe, the champion trash talker this morning, acting as Sam's loudest fan. Sam stands in a carefully rehearsed batting stance: feet spread slightly apart, knees bent, butt sticking out, back elbow up, front elbow in, head locked in on the pitcher. After two strikes, the third pitch is over his head, and Sam ducks out of the way, ball one.

It's suddenly pretty loud on *Waramaug* ball field. The office staff way out past center field is probably wondering what all the ruckus is about. Down the left-field line, in his cottage, surely Waboos has heard these cheers before. Many years earlier, Waboos was the heart and soul of the staff team that played once a summer against the Moose campers in baseball.

The ten-year-old pitcher winds up in that exaggerated way, imitative of whatever pitcher he's seen on television, and grooves a pitch across the plate. Sam swings, and an unexpected soft ping of the bat is heard. The ball rolls out about two feet in front of the plate and settles in the dirt. There's about a tenth of a second of complete silence and stillness, forty campers and staff, Sam included, all staring at the ball, which is sitting no more than twenty-five inches in front of the plate. Then, chaos: campers yelling at Sam to drop the bat and run, the other team yelling at their catcher to pick up the ball. Sam is thrown out at first by about three steps, and the inning is over. He stops at first base, standing on top of the bag, probably not entirely sure what has just happened, and probably also relishing the feeling of standing on the base with a batting helmet on. He's out. The teams are jogging off and on to change sides, but Sam stands for another second on first base, smiling widely.

If Help the Other Fellow is motto number one at Camp Keewaydin, then Be a Fair Winner and a Good Loser is motto number two. Both mottoes hang on pennants in Waboos's office.

Granted, messages are hard to communicate to kids, especially youngsters the age of *Waramaug* campers. And Be a Fair Winner and a Good Loser is not as powerful as a message as Vince Lombardi's "Winning isn't everything— it's the only thing." Kids are brought up in a culture that emphasizes winning and losing, especially with regard to sports. Pepe is a seasoned trash talker because he's been watching professional athletes on television for years. There's really nothing wrong with this, per se, as professional athletes are paid to win. And no one can argue that winning, in sports or anything in life, isn't fun. Winning is in many ways the most powerful confirmation of hard work, dedication, focus, and desire.

What is important, though, is that despite the many benefits of winning, knowing how to lose is also important. Winning is rare and elusive, while losing is painful and common. One must know how to deal with adversity, control oneself in times of discomfort, and value the elements of competition that are ultimately necessary for either fair winning or good losing.

I learned all this not during my days in business but at Keewaydin.

A sports team or a business could win on talent alone, but in truth it usually takes more than that. And these other, clichéd attributes—teamwork, dedication to a common goal, attitude—are the facets of competition that Keewaydin emphasizes most strongly. I have never seen such a close group of people as I did with the assembled group of hockey players in the locker room after the Mighty Ducks lost in the finals of the Stanley Cup in 2003. They had lost with honor, having been underdogs all season, and had gone much further than anybody expected. Winning is important, but so is losing if it brings the team together. Ultimately, losing can teach you how to win.

camp

After the baseball game, a similar *Waramaug* crew returns to the basketball court for a free-time game. Things are progressing pretty much as they did this morning, with some reckless play and disputed fouls and arguments, before one of the wigwam staffmen comes over to the game and decides that he'll join.

He refigures the teams to make them more evenly matched, and immediately institutes a "three passes before you can shoot" rule to ensure everyone gets involved in the action. Soon, the tide of the game has changed dramatically. Q still dominates, even sneaking by the staffman a few times for razzle-dazzle layups. Pepe continues to spot up shots from the outside, but he also plays a little defense when egged on by the staffman. By the end of the game, everyone's gotten involved in the action, skilled and unskilled players alike, and, oddly enough, when the gong rings for dinner, the campers are having such a good time that no one remembers what the score is. Nobody knows which team has won, and nobody seems to care.

Does this example mean that Q, Pepe, and their friends will never engage in trash talking again? Does it mean that they will know from now on to focus on being a fair winner and a good loser? I don't think so. I think that is unrealistic, given their age and natural lack of maturity. When the boys are ready, the message will stick.

A small start has been made.

chapter ten

license to drive

1958

When I was sixteen years old, I got my driver's license; I was free. I was off to my first job: going to work as a Keewaydin staffman. This time, I didn't go to Grand Central Station with my parents to catch the train to camp. Instead, I just walked out of my father's house in Bedford Hills, strolled around the front of the 1950 Chrysler that my grandparents were discarding, threw my bag full of camp shirts, underwear, and socks in the trunk, and headed for Keewaydin. It was the same drive I had first taken nine years earlier with my father.

My mother, in typical fashion, had gotten detailed maps from the automobile club and had prepared a full three-course lunch, placed in a paper bag on the seat next to me for my survival. Clear instructions to call when I arrived had been hammered into my head. I was off.

I drove fast; all sixteen-year-old males with two-week-old licenses drive too fast. In Chappaqua, just ten miles from my house, I was pulled over by a police officer. He yelled at me, and gave me a ticket. He never asked my age, which was at once exhilarating and a little humiliating. He didn't question whether I was old enough to drive. After threatening to "take me in," he let me go on, confident for some reason that he had convinced me to "slow down." And come to think of it, he had . . . until I got to Bridgeport.

Sometimes people in pickup trucks drive too slowly, I convinced myself as I changed radio stations and loped along on Route 7, stuck behind one of those pickups. I wanted to get on with it, to move on, to push to Keewaydin, and so I passed him. Now I was singing Buddy Holly songs, the June wind was blowing through my grandmother's coupe, and then someone passed me. It struck me as the insult of all time, being passed when you're sixteen and driving to your job. I gave up the music and returned to concentrating on the road. I approached another truck that was going too slowly, and so I did what I had to do: I passed him, too. This was no four-lane highway, mind you, just two curvy lanes, driving under old-fashioned conditions, when zero to sixty had real meaning.

The road continued as I moved from town to town, on occasion hitting those annoying red lights. Coming out of Bridgeport, I was passed again, but this time, eyes and ears on the road, I was ready, and I quickly remembered the pass, accelerating toward Hartford, all the while keeping one hand in the paper sack to my right, rummaging for the potato chips.

camp

As I came into the first stop sign in Hartford, I noticed in my rearview mirror (something I had rarely used in my vast experience of driving) a familiar truck, with the driver giving me an all-too-familiar middle finger. Seemed odd, yes, but understandable, since this was the truck I had passed back in Bridgeport. His door started to swing open just as I pulled away. Then it closed. I wondered what that was all about.

Now, suddenly, this truck was inches behind me, inches at forty miles an hour. Now it was coming clear: I had passed this pickup truck three times—the same one. Suddenly, I was studying the rearview mirror, and I almost ran off the road and over a dog. Now I got it. In the truck was one mean-looking guy. A car in front of me stopped at a red light, leaving me no option but to brake as well. Behind me, a door swung open, the driver leaving his truck and approaching my grandmother's suddenly stuffy green car. I think I stopped breathing. As he walked up to my car, I closed the window and locked the car. The light didn't change and the car in front of me wouldn't move.

I kept from gazing to my left. All I could hear was muffled expletives—and words like *kid, brat, punk,* and then the alarming sound of one of my windows shattering. Then the light turned green and I was moving forward, my shaking foot somehow finding the gas pedal. He turned away, having spent his anger, and as he became a vision in the rearview mirror, I took a breath.

I drove five more hours, never more than five miles over the speed limit. I arrived at camp about 10:00 P.M. with a broken window, an injured sense of maturity, and a story that I wouldn't tell my parents for at least five years.

I hadn't seen Waboos in a long time, having taken a break from Keewaydin when I was too old to be a camper and too young to be a staffman. When he approached me, it wasn't as the young kid I felt like, but as a staffman. "Hey, Mike, glad you're with us," and then, walking away, he added, "Oh, by the way, you're in Moose. I think Jim Fullerton is up the mountain."

I was in Moose! I was in Moose? After a long day, I was stunned and speechless. The *Moosalamoo* wigwam was for the oldest kids, the fourteen- and fifteen-year-olds, up on Mount Moosalamoo, across Keewaydin Road. I was uneasy, even a little confused, but also honored to be put in with the most senior trippers.

Waboos had vanished into the night. I took it that I had been instructed to go up the mountain to find Jim Fullerton, the head of *Moosalamoo*. Jim effortlessly ran Moose in the summer and the Brown University hockey team in the winter. He was a winner in both places.

I was about to start my first job; I had worked in a hospital the summer before, but without pay. This was my first real earning position. Firsts are hard. You can spend your entire life walking into new situations, from the first day of kindergarten to the first day of college, a first toast at a wedding to a first funeral, first kiss to the first day of your child's life. We learn to deal with firsts. Each is hard, some easier than the ones before. Climbing Mount Moosalamoo in the dark to meet my boss for the first time after a long drive remains up there as a hard first.

I started the climb, a weak flashlight from my car in hand. Four times, I was convinced I had lost the trail and would soon come across some unknown cave that held the bones of a missing hiker. Behind every tree, I imagined some wild animal lurked. Chipmunks became rats; roots became snakes.

I arrived. Jim was sleeping. There were a few other bodies sleeping in the bunks, other staffmen who had already arrived. I lay down and studied what I could see of the bunk over my head. Suddenly being sixteen didn't seem so old, and being a staffman for kids almost my own age seemed overwhelming. I didn't remember Jim Fullerton snoring so loud a couple summers earlier. Meanwhile, his German shepherd kept rolling over, and I heard every grunt from both ends of that dog. I wondered where that truck driver was now, and where that angry policeman might be. I then started worrying about the rest of the staff being hundreds of years older than I was, and I was quickly getting less and less excited about the hike up that mountain every day for eight weeks.

All that kept me awake for what seemed like hours, though it was probably more like ten minutes.

The morning light was welcome; everything, if only for an instant, seemed much simpler and easier in the light. Jim was delighted to see me. The other ancient staff, at least twenty-five years old, greeted me as they would a younger camper, though it did seem they were happy to see me. The daylight couldn't completely ease my mood; I was still overwhelmed by the day before. We all walked down to breakfast together to begin getting the wigwam ready for the arrival of the campers.

After breakfast, the familiar figure of a man with a duck walk came across campus. I had seen Waboos at breakfast, off at the other end of the dining hall. I'd caught his eye several times, but we hadn't talked. He was busy, running things that needed to be run. Now he came toward me. I couldn't see anybody else around whom he could be heading to. He kept coming and then stopped in front of me.

"You didn't seem to be talking too much this morning," he said to me. That was odd. How did he know that? "Everything okay?"

"Yeah, sure," was my response. And then it slipped out. "Do you think I'm too young to work in *Moosalamoo*?"

"You are a little young for that. I guess you're just a year or so older than some of the other kids. Let's put you in *Wiantinaug*."

"Great," I said. And that was that. Waboos knew right away what I was feeling, what I was thinking. He understood. I went to work with the kids who were twelve and thirteen, and had the most wonderful summer. At the end, as I was leaving, Waboos came up with my hundred-dollar check for the summer's work.

camp

"I'm glad we decided that you shouldn't work in Moose," he said. "That probably would have been a mistake, though you could have handled it."

I thanked Waboos and left for Bedford Hills. I drove carefully and didn't pass any trucks along the way.

chapter eleven

the lengthened shadow

present

At lunchtime, a meal gong sounds. All activity ceases—in tents, in forts, on fields—and the campers swarm in a collective rush toward the dining hall. Some of the younger campers choose to sprint, some of the more distracted (or less hungry) kids walk absentmindedly, and some of the older kids do nothing, at least for a few minutes, too cool to be part of the mad rush.

The staffmen at the doors hold a new weapon—waterless hand-soap. Each entering camper, staffman, and visitor gets a squirt in the hand. They pass inside through this human checkpoint and through the open wooden screen doors, scores of hand pairs rubbing together.

It is then he walks into the dining hall, or, rather, is walked in, today by daughter Laurie. In the summer, his whole family has traditionally been together again, the family that started here. This year, the kids are all here—Laurie in from Seattle, Peter up from Philly, and Steve just down the road from the health club he owns—only their mother is absent. She is not well, and her absence at camp is noticeable.

Laurie escorts her father to a familiar spot, aptly numbered Table 1, then to a familiar chair at the end of the table, a camper on each side and a *Waramaug* staffman directly across.

"Who's going to go up and get the lunch meat? . . . Okay, good, you can go."

"Where is the pitcher of juice? Where is the water? . . . Okay, pass the water around starting here, the juice around starting there."

He doesn't seem to know the names of the faceless campers around him, yet he still indicates some understanding and recollection of their personalities. "Oh, that's right, you don't like milk. Well, I know you're the one who didn't like syrup at breakfast, and you don't like mayonnaise; you like your food plain!"

After the meal has been eaten, a camper waiting the table takes the dishes and glasses back into the kitchen and returns with apples for dessert. The bowl of Macintoshes is placed in front of Waboos, and no one seems sure what to do next. There aren't enough for the whole table; they'll need to be cut in pieces.

As if he could see the problem himself, Waboos asks the camper next to him for a knife. He feels for and grabs one of the apples from the bowl and begins slicing it. The first slice is made, and then Waboos, in a swooping movement, impales it with the knife and holds it out for the camper next to him, who grabs the apple slice from the knife and takes a bite. Another impaled slice is held out for the next camper, and so forth. Even the other staffer at the table reaches across to Waboos and grabs a slice off the knife.

What's most intriguing about all this—aside from the tableau of the blind octogenarian holding apple slices out for campers with his knife—is that during the whole scene, which goes on for about fifteen minutes, nothing is said. The camper chatter ceases; Table 1 is silent amid the sounds of neighboring lunchers. It is almost as if the ten-year-olds are reflecting as they eat about the history of the process. Waboos has cut apples like this for generations of Table 1 residents, for hundreds, if not thousands, of campers.

To understand who this man is at this camp, why he is such an icon, one must travel far back in time, decades earlier, when my father and uncles canoed, swam, and played as young men. And during those days, those years, some seven decades ago, the camper with that funny name, Waboos, kept coming back, summer after summer after summer. Soon the legend would be created that the little kid named Waboos was either born in one of the green *Annwi* cabins or perhaps had lived there permanently ever since he was four years old.

Indeed, with his practically white head of hair and joyful spirit, the boy was well known and well liked at the camp, and he became a fixture on Lake Dunmore, returning summer after summer through the 1920s and 1930s, progressing from the youngest *Annwi* wigwam through

Moosalamoo and onto the Keewaydin staff. There, he made his closest friends, had his best memories. Meanwhile, the camp continued to grow under the guidance of director Sid Negus, who not only set the tone for the camp but also improved its facilities, adding a boxing ring, new cabins, and more.

In 1938, the expanded greater Keewaydin Camps, Ltd.—with camps in Maine, Florida, and elsewhere—ran short of resources. The corporation dissolved, and each camp got a new, independent owner. For Keewaydin Dunmore, it was a man by the name of Speedy Rush, who by default became its director as well as its proprietor. After fourteen years as director, the icon of the camp, Sid Negus, had left Lake Dunmore.

Speedy Rush stayed on as camp director for five years, before financial pressures led him to investigate selling the camp in the early 1940s. With many of the loyal young staff away in Europe and the Pacific, fighting in World War II, Keewaydin was suddenly in some danger. Fortunately, thanks to an unlikely reunion overseas, the camp was soon to find enthusiastic suitors.

In Paris, in the spring of 1945, Waboos was in an army unit near the city, and Abby Fenn—a fellow Keewaydin *Papoosiwog,* or veteran—was in the air force, stationed in England. One night, flying across the Channel, Abby's plane had mechanical trouble and his squadron was forced to spend the night in Paris. Via some phone calls and a bit of investigating, Abby discovered that Waboos was due to be at the Grand Hotel at 11:00 P.M. Sure enough, as he retold it years later, while Abby stood outside the hotel waiting, a soldier approached out of the darkness, with a familiar gait and a customary pipe in his mouth.

"Waboos?" Abby asked. The soldier did a double take—as Abby described it years later, "a proper reaction from a man who hadn't expected to hear 'Waboos' come out of the pitch-darkness of Paris."

That night, Abby told Waboos of the sale situation at Keewaydin, and that he and Slim Curtiss—another peer at camp—had already discussed buying the camp themselves but didn't have sufficient money for a down payment. According to some rough calculations done in the dark, it seemed that Waboos could make up the difference. They agreed to investigate the situation and to approach Speedy Rush when they got back to the United States.

Soon, Speedy, who had been reluctantly entertaining offers from outsiders, decided to sell the camp to the Waboos-Abby-Slim triumvirate for considerably less than he was offering Keewaydin to the other bidders, and just like that, the camp had three new owners, all prepared to continue the camp's legacy. The story reminds me now of *White Christmas,* when Bing Crosby puts on a show to save the hotel while singing one of the most famous songs ever written, one of Irving Berlin's best.

"Keewaydin has meant that which is the most inspiring and the happiest and the best in my life. Keewaydin is the great ideal realized, and much of the credit must go to Waboos Hare."

michael d. eisner

This is an excerpt from a letter written by Richard Garnett, included in a collection of such tributes at a celebration commemorating Waboos's sixtieth anniversary at the camp in 1983. The celebration took place at a fall reunion, with perhaps the most special of Waboos's gifts that day being an album full of letters and tributes from seven decades and multiple generations of campers, alumni, and parents. Richard Garnett's letter was included in this album, which now, still in great condition, rests in my lap as I sit across the desk from Waboos in Hare House, the small cottage on the edge of *Waramaug* ball field. In the middle of my second visit to Keewaydin—a few weeks into the summer—I'm trying to determine what it is that has made Waboos such a legend at Keewaydin, and what has made me return to camp this summer to spend time with him. What has happened since my first meeting with him—when he called my father "Les" and put me in a boxing ring with a boy twice my size—that had left me so bewildered? Why did I care?

"We never ceased to wonder," wrote Doc Mather in his 1983 letter, "at how quickly you learned the names of all the boys and at your efforts to make sure all of them understood the 'Keewaydin Spirit.'"

It really is a wonder that the man could remember the names of every child in camp, and always knew what to say. "How's the K-stroke coming, Timmy?" to a boy about to get his first coup in canoeing. "Nice hit today, Richie," to a *Waramaug* camper who had played baseball in the morning. Even more so to parents—parents who could barely introduce themselves on midseason visits before Waboos would give them a full report on their son's summer, putting them at ease quickly.

"Oh yes, you must be the Stauffers, from Hershey," George Stauffer, a camper in 1960 and later a Columbia University professor, remembered Waboos telling his parents. "Your son, George? He's having a great time, I think I just saw him up on the ball field. His team's leading, four to two. Why don't you have a look at the campus until the game's over. It should be finished in twenty minutes or so."

Today, Waboos can't see a face, yet he still produces a name. His camera has lost its focus in the last few years, yet he still remembers. At opening day a few weeks ago, outside his cabin, a crowd of people huddled together around Waboos, like the fans around the celebrity of honor at a banquet.

"Waboos, it's Tom Atkinson, from Armonk. I was at camp from 1968 to 1970. My son Tommy is in *Wiantinaug* this summer."

"Right, Tom. *Wiantinaug.* Great tennis player. Still playing?"

Tom Atkinson, being reduced to a young camper again, is giddy that Waboos remembered him, his tennis skills, just one camper in thousands that have come through. I think Waboos remembers me now by my voice. I only see him once every few years.

Clare Curtin, who was a wigwam leader when I was on staff, summed up what it was like working with Waboos.

"I emphasize working *with,* for, being a staffman at Keewaydin, I felt that there was never a sense of being made to work *for* Waboos."

Staffers decades later still recall the notes that Waboos would leave in their small mailboxes in the camp office. "Nice job running the Frolic last week; your wigwam's skits were terrific!—Waboos." "Good job handling the fight between your campers during rest hour today. You did the right thing.—Waboos." His ability and willingness to trust empowered us as staffers to do our jobs confidently and to do them well. And thus, for many of us who had also been campers, the benevolent yet mysterious and powerful director was transformed instantly into a winning, approachable, and likable boss—a striking paradox in some ways, but very logical for those who knew him summer after summer.

Getting a note from Waboos as a staffman was a moment of excitement for me, a real motivation to do better, a real lift. And I never forgot it. Getting such a note from the president of ABC in the 1970s when I didn't think he knew my name was similarly exhilarating. And, conversely, somehow being admonished by Waboos wasn't a lasting indictment.

In his cottage, I continue to flip through the pages of the album. The letters are full of memories, anecdotes, and jokes, recollections of years of tradition, with Waboos in the middle of it all.

I find, surprisingly, a letter from my father, in which he notes that he had known Waboos for "but one year short of his sixty years at Keewaydin." He wrote also that "today, when we sit together with our friends and family at camp-fire in the *Wiantinaug* circle, we have that wonderful feeling of 'returning.' Keewaydin remains, as it has always been, a sea of tranquility in a tumultuous world. In no small way, Waboos has made it so." It's more insight on why my father never missed a camp reunion.

Scrolling through the whole album, a clearer picture emerges with each new letter. For those who found spirituality and tranquility at Keewaydin, Waboos was the symbol of those attributes. For those who found Keewaydin a place of refuge and comfort for years, Waboos was the one who made them feel most comfortable, or at least symbolized this comfort. For those who remember Keewaydin for the empowerment they got when they learned how to canoe, or hit a home run in a baseball game, or write the Sunday *Kicker,* Waboos is the one they remember lauding them. For staff members who recall Keewaydin as an institution they loved and passionately strove to make their imprint upon each summer, Waboos was the one who directed these passions, who encouraged them. For my father, who saw Keewaydin as a piece of tradition passed through the generations of his family, a place to which he was sent a few months after his mother had died, Waboos was its caretaker.

My own letter, on Paramount Pictures stationery, supports this notion; I wrote that "Keewaydin may have been the single most important educational experience for me for what I do today." Like all these other Keewaydinese folks I joined in the album, my letter to Waboos was a thank-you note to him for being the central component of what I treasured—the figure who offered me this unique education—from my Keewaydin experience.

Not surprisingly, the short letter from John McPhee puts it best. "Waboos," he concluded, "you are what they who boast Keewaydin mean."

In 1946, the three owners quickly settled upon very different roles. Slim soon began running the summer school at Sidwell Friends in Washington, D.C., and became to us campers, at least, a silent partner, only seen on rare occasions.

Abby, officially the associate director, showed a passion for the grounds and facilities of Keewaydin. Later, he developed other programs: the seven-week Wilderness trip program for older Keewaydin campers, much of it led by Indian guides; nature camps for troubled kids in Florida; weeklong programs for Middlebury schoolchildren during the fall to learn about nature and the ecosystem at Keewaydin. He was also the wigwam director of *Wiantinaug* for many years.

Clearly evolving as the heart of the camp leadership, though, was Waboos. While his partners ably handled business decisions for the camp, he, as the sole director, threw himself into the heart of the operations—leading the staff and guiding the campers. He modeled his approach to camp leadership after his mentor, Sid Negus, but quickly made his own mark. He goofily led song sessions after dinner; he solemnly led the opening Four Winds Ceremony during the first week of camp; he happily orchestrated the Sunday *Kicker* festivities at the *Wiantinaug* campfires. He sat in the front row at Friday Night Frolics; he took the calls from concerned parents and settled disputes between unruly campers. He was everywhere and anywhere for the summer's eight weeks.

Looking back, I suppose that as a young *Waramaug* camper, I never gave much thought to the idea that Waboos might have a life outside of camp. Much as children never consider the fact that their teachers don't live at school, none of us ever considered that Waboos didn't actually live the entire year in his cabin, eating at the dining hall by himself while we were back home. We never gave much thought to the idea that home for him was suburban Philadelphia, and that his winters were spent not at Keewaydin but at the Montgomery School as a middle school teacher and sports coach. There, he was Alfred Hare, or Mr. Hare to his students.

The arrival of Katie Hare—Mrs. Waboos—came during my fourth summer at Keewaydin, 1953. Women were not part of the fabric of Keewaydin, at least in the mind of an eight- or ten-year-old. They worked as nurses in the dispensary, as well as in the kitchen, in the office, and in the laundry. They were the wives of senior staffmen and also cared for their young children, mostly parenting at the wives' dock. Nobody knew where they slept or ate, though there was a sense there were some tents "over there." I never knew that the wives ate a half-hour before we did, or that there was one fort, called "Inwigo," exclusively for the women.

Yet one summer, suddenly Mrs. Waboos showed up. The main change was that Waboos and his wife moved into the Bug House—the camp's original nature conservatory. It's along the path beside the lake, between *Waramaug* and *Wiantinaug*—a pretty high-traffic location—and you could always look in. Pretty soon, there were new additions to the family: Steve, Laurie, and then Peter. All in the two-room tiny cottage that used to be the Bug House. The greatest irony, I always thought, was that none of the beds was ever made. Each morning, we spent a half-hour perfecting the corners on our own sheets for inspection, and yet the beds in the director's cabin were disheveled.

Marriage must have been a big change in Waboos's life. He now had a wife and then three children, but to all of us there was no change except for this woman named Katie who floated through camp, planting and attending to the flower beds. She moved among the trees and through the grass like an actress on the stage wearing a large hoop-skirt, obscuring any legs that might be there, smiling and saying hello as she drifted by, her small children often in tow. Waboos never really seemed as attached to any of them as to us. He was still there at every meal at Table 1 with six campers and another staffman.

The idea that I did not think about Waboos's life as Alfred Hare's is on my mind as I take a firm grip of Waboos's elbow on this humid summer day and lead him down the sloping hill beyond his cabin to my rental car. For, in fact, we are leaving camp and going to a place where he is Alfred, his condo up the road in Middlebury. I help him into the Ford Explorer, almost having to lift him up onto the seat, and we begin driving.

We talk about his wife, albeit a bit uncomfortably. I don't know much more than I did when I was eleven. She is not here this summer, and she does not live with Waboos in his condo, instead spending her days in a home in Philadelphia. "It's better this way," says Waboos quietly. I don't ask any more questions.

We guide each other into the condo, which is in a small development off Middlebury's main road. The door is unlocked, so we walk right in. On the window seat, he is Alfred—pictures of his family, of his kids through the years. On the rest of the walls, he remains as I know him—Waboos. Waboos in the 1930s and 1940s, a vigorous young man with a hearty smile. Waboos in the 1950s and 1960s as camp director, a pipe in his mouth. Waboos in the 1970s and 1980s, flanked by Slim and Abby. Waboos can't see the pictures anymore; I describe a picture, and then he explains where it was taken, when it was taken. He wants to show me the rest of the condo—his bedroom (naturally, the bed isn't made), the kitchen—but I'm much more comfortable scanning the walls where he remains Waboos than those where he is Alfred, a regular family man in regular family portraits.

There it is! On the wall, by his desk in the corner, a small picture: "the one I have been telling you about, Waboos." I had heard that this picture was now in his condo, and this is why I am really here, to find it. First, it had hung in Waboos's cottage by the lake at camp, and then for years it had been in the Rec Cabin up on Mount Moosalamoo. I always dragged my wife up the mountain to see it, and my kids, and once even my mother, a big hike simply to see a picture.

I went back again and it was gone, though not for long. It was in Hare House for a time, but the spot where it hung now was empty. Somehow, the rumor was true. It had made its way north on Route 7 to Waboos's condo. On a rock, Sid Negus is posed with about a dozen campers, Waboos and my father included. They are all about ten years old, all sitting on rocks after swimming in the Cascades way up Mount Moosalamoo, a small stream with mini-waterfalls and freezing water. There's Waboos, at ten years old, surely not knowing that he would own this rock in twenty years, and remain near it for another sixty. And there's my father, not knowing that he would have a son who would sit on that very same rock someday, much less four grandsons who would also sit on the very same rock. There it is, and there is my father again looking out at me, ten years old, with his life in front of him.

This was the picture that connected me to the opening scene in *Dead Poets Society* when I read the script that later became a Robin Williams motion picture, in particular the scene when Williams shows his students pictures of classes long ago graduated, pictures of men now ancient. As Williams's character notes in the movie, the boys in those pictures—just like these boys—are in the prime of their youth, the starting line of their life, everything ahead of them. This was when I was first moved by carpe diem.

Here is Waboos, here is my father, eighty years ago looking forward to something they knew not.

The ride home is quiet as I think about the picture I borrowed, now in the trunk, to be copied later and put on my desk in California. Suddenly, Waboos asks, "Why is there a brown river flowing down the street?"

"What do you mean?" I reply. "What do you see? Is it the yellow line in the middle of the road?"

"No, I can make that out," he said. "On the side of the road, though, I see all this brown, a brown river, with, I think, leaves all around, leaves in brownish orange colors."

The road is bordered at this point with nothing but green grass.

"It must be my eyes," he says. "I'm not sure which one. The doctors said there would be changes at some point, that I might start to see things, the light making its way through."

"Maybe that's it," I say. "Maybe this is the start of some progress." Two detached retinas—maybe there is more light yet in store for his life. I want to be positive.

"No, but there are no brown leaves in the summer," he concludes remorsefully after a short silence. "My eyes are just fooling me." He seems resigned. "In my heart I think I'll see again, but in my head I know I'm blind.

"It's all brown," he repeats quietly to himself. "It's all brown."

At the start of the twenty-first century, Waboos Hare spends his days ushered around by those he himself guided throughout the twentieth century. Abby Fenn lives nearby and takes him to dinner several times a week during the winter, and other senior staffmen sit with him in Hare House during summer afternoons, leading his eyes to the right parts of pictures of days past. (Sadly, Slim Curtiss died a few years ago.) Waboos's children, who like to call him Wa-Dad, as he signed his notes to them, are all near the camp in the summer, with the youngest one, Peter, the successor to his father's legacy as camp director. Staffmen, some old, some new, all revere him either as the legendary leader they have known for years or as the iconic relic he proudly remains today. Campers are in awe of a man who has been around so long, who knows so much. Alumni, many of whom are now parents of campers, circle him at visitor days. He is a piece of history, the treasured ambassador of the past who reminds us what we should be in the present.

In his famous essay "Self-Reliance," Ralph Waldo Emerson wrote that "an institution is the lengthened shadow of one man." It is the shadow of Waboos that casts itself upon Keewaydin.

In the car, I remain silent, a bit stunned by the poetry of the tricks that Waboos's eyes are playing on him. I want to break the silence. I want to make sure he knows that there is no brown on the side of the road, that it's all green, and that the leaves are safely nestled in the trees. I want to tell him that it's still summer.

He may be almost ninety, he may be increasingly immobile, and he may be blind. He may be lonely in his condo, and he may be thinking about his wife lying confused, sick, and lost on a bed in a nursing home somewhere far away, in Philadelphia.

But I want him to know that here, at Lake Dunmore, it's still summer. I speed up the car, pushing the accelerator farther down, almost out of instinct. I want to get back to camp faster, want to return this man, Alfred Hare, who sits in my passenger seat, return him to summer, to his home, to Keewaydin. Where there is no brown. Where all the leaves are in the trees. Where the flowers that his wife once planted still bloom.

Where he is alive.

chapter twelve

men at work

1960

The first time I realized I was being talked to like an adult was my freshman year at college. It was quite by accident. I was sitting in an auditorium, listening to the dean lecture to all the incoming freshmen. He said, "Men, this is a very important day, and . . ." I heard nothing else. Who was he talking to? And then I realized it was us, us boys, us boys sitting there listening to what life would be like at college. I heard nothing else because the word men kept ringing through my head. It was awesome, scary, unreal, and not about us. He must have been talking to another group. I kept fixating on his use of the word men until he got to the part about pornography. Yes, pornography! Equating reading Chaucer and Shakespeare and history and psychology and chemistry to pornography brought my attention back. "Don't tell me, men," he said, "that you cannot read quickly and comprehend what you read. Don't tell me, men, you cannot fully understand a philosophy assignment. Don't tell me Kierkegaard is complicated. I'm sure you read *Playboy* quickly. I'm sure you can read *Fanny Hill* quickly and understand every bit of it."

As he kept talking, the word *Playboy* receded in my mind and the word *men* again preoccupied me. It was the first time someone else had referred to me as a man, and it couldn't be true. We were still boys, high school boys. We didn't have to worry about food or lodging or clothes; we were still simply boys, sent away. But as the dean concluded his speech, I realized for the first time that I was beginning my life on my own, under my own control. College was something I had elected to do. I was about to pass through the second and most important stage of adolescence: growing up and being independent.

The following summer was my second as a staffman. I was placed in *Wiantinaug*, in the same tent as the previous year, Tent 10. I was still a junior staffman, full of excitement, and other staffmen usually told me what to do, which was fine with me. I was a willing follower. And then Abby Fenn asked me to drive the truck carrying eight campers and two staffmen and five canoes in tow to the Rangeley Lakes in Maine, a six-hour drive. This trip originated in Salisbury, Vermont, at the camp, and the group had to be driven to where we "put in" six hours north. All the duffel bags, wanagans, tents, shovels, axes, and canoes—plus ten people—had to be transported to the Rangeley Lakes. It was like a war movie in my mind. Ten soldiers in the back of a truck, sitting in rows, about to be driven off to their adventure, pulling a trailer of five canoes. I would be the driver.

I'd had a license for two years. And only since March had I been allowed to drive in New York City, or at night anywhere in New York State. The truck had a stick shift, with about a hundred gears, plus the canoes in tow.

"Do you know how to drive a truck?" Abby asked. "Yes, I do," I responded, which was somewhat true, since I could drive a very small Chevy stick-shift truck on my grandfather's farm. Just like that, I was driving the campers on their trip.

A few years earlier, I hadn't been a safe driver, but on this trip I rose to the occasion. As I drove—as I drove oh so carefully—all that was running through my mind was how crazy the camp was, letting this boy drive eight campers and two staffmen for six hours on back roads in Vermont and Maine. And meanwhile, they were singing in the back, and talking and planning their trip. Not once did they wonder about their safety in that truck. But I did. I got them there safely, and I drove back. I drove back to Vermont proud, excited, amazed. When I pulled into camp and put the parking brake on, I felt like I had joined a new club, though I couldn't quite figure out exactly what that club was. It was midnight when I got back to Dunmore, and I wanted to find somebody else who was in the club I had just joined, just to share the moment.

But everybody was asleep.

The feeling of being in that club, feeling like a member of something, very adult, disappeared pretty quickly when I returned to my junior staffman routines. It passed silently until the second month of that summer.

"Mike," Abby said to me this time, "we'd like you to lead our first trip down the Connecticut River, starting in Canada and ending up at the bridge in Lancaster [New Hampshire]."

In my two seasons on staff, I had actually only led one trip before, a simple trip that had been done hundreds of times in New England. This Connecticut River trip was new. The camp had almost no records about the area. There would be rapids and portaging and nobody senior to me. Once again, I heard myself immediately saying yes. I thought I could do it, but at the same time I was overcome by the awareness that they were allowing me to take a trip that had never been taken before.

We left. We had eight of the best trippers in *Wiantinaug* and a great second staffman. We organized the trip to perfection. Every meal was planned, which is standard, but staying up in the dining hall late, surrounded by maps and journals of previous trips, I planned every other detail as well, over and over. I made sure every tent was perfect, that our maps were the most up-to-date, that canned ham was included, and that the first-aid kit was checked and rechecked.

Confident but anxious, I was ready.

The trip was wonderful for the first four days. We ran the rapids. We poled down the river. We forged campsites and portaged around the falls on the river. On the fourth day, the canoe with twelve-year-old John Joy in the bow raced up ahead on the river and hid in the weeds along the shore. When the other four canoes arrived at the spot where John Joy's canoe was hiding, out flew his canoe from the weeds as the other boys yelled war chants and howled with laughter. John's canoe was foolishly floating backward during this mock battle, when it suddenly entered the rapids and took off, hitting a boulder that sent John flying out of the canoe headfirst, where he landed on hard rocks jutting out of the river.

I jumped into the river, pulled John out, and made it to the shore. There was blood everywhere in sight. He was a mess but totally conscious and coherent. Nonetheless, a head wound, even a superficial one, can be very bloody.

We regrouped on the shore. The other seven campers and one staffman decided to create a campsite there while I carried John to safety. I looked at the map and went off the trail heading in the direction where I thought there would be civilization. I eventually found an empty dirt road. I trekked maybe three miles, carrying John the whole way, before a car finally drove past. Inside was a local farmer, and he took us to the nearest hospital, where they sewed up John. He was fine, although scared, but not as scared as I was. A member of the hospital staff drove us back to the campsite and we continued the trip.

Over the last few days of that trip, as it became clear that John Joy was okay and that we had triumphed over adversity once again, I felt like I had fully joined the club of true team leaders, of adults. It was as if the truck drive had been an initiation, and now I had passed the true membership test. I had matured. I had become one of the men whom the dean had spoken of almost a year earlier. I had performed well under fire. John and I agreed we would never tell anybody how he had come to fall out of that canoe—because, in fact, it was *my* canoe that had fallen into the rapids. I was John's partner—riding in the stern. Floating backward downriver had been my foolish idea.

After the trip, I failed a big test. On several occasions, I almost went to see Abby to tell him what had really happened, to explain that it was my canoe and my irresponsibility that had caused the accident. But telling the truth proved harder to do than walking three miles with a twelve-year-old in my arms. I didn't do it, even though deep inside I realized that telling the full truth would have made me feel much more like the person I wanted to be— or, to be honest, feel more like the man I wanted to be. I wasn't ready. I wasn't mature enough then. I just couldn't admit it. Years later, I told Abby what had really happened on that trip. By then, we all treated my account as an amusing story. Yet it wasn't. I had realized that becoming a man is a continual process; no matter how easily the dean had used the word *men*, it was still only a temporary pass.

chapter thirteen

the four winds ceremony

1963

I was a Keewaydin staffman for four summers, each time in *Wiantinaug,* firmly entrenched in Tent 10. This tent sat with its back to the ball field and its front facing the path into the *Wiantinaug* campus of fourteen other tents. If the tent flaps were up—as they almost always were during the day—our tent became the best place to monitor who was walking in and out of the wigwam. My immediate responsibility was to oversee the four campers whose cots surrounded mine inside the tent, though we spent most parts of the day outside.

While I had originally learned much as a camper—skills of teamwork, self-reliance, initiative, leadership—I picked up much more during my years as a staffman. It is during those years—roughly from age seventeen to age twenty-two—when a person goes through what I think of as a second adolescence, where a life is finally molded into action. It is during those years when school is no longer required, and when you start to plan where to work, where to live, with whom to spend your life. It is during those years that you figure out your path.

For me, the Keewaydin experience as a staffman helped set my course through this second adolescence. I had been through challenging times on trips, and now I was more comfortable with the responsibilities that came along with my duties as a staffman. The summer before, two years following the episode with John Joy, I was hiking through a thunderstorm on Mount Mansfield with four campers. Instead of moving up to our campsite with some danger of lightning, we hiked downhill, following a river torrent, and ended up in a motel for the night. Though very wet, we stayed out of real danger. It was another instance on a trip when I was pressured to be responsible for making a decision for others. Flexibility became part of leadership. This was a new experience, a first of its kind. These moments were like driving on a highway for the first time (as small as that seems today), or writing a big term paper for the first time (still an unpleasant thought). A celebrated event, a big milestone in life, but then, as you do it over and over again, it simply becomes part of your life.

Life after dark for staffmen was centered in the dining hall. The trips were planned there, letters written, and the modest social life took place there. I had become the sort of staffman that others approached in the dining hall late at night when planning their trips, looking for clues and tips on different routes, or advice on what to do in different situations. Like anyone else at that age—high school, college—the community of Keewaydin staffmen looked up to experience, even if the experienced one was quite young.

camp

In the days before Songadeewin relocated to Lake Dunmore, there were almost no girls on the lake, and thus no female staff for miles. These days at camp, after the campers go to bed, the staffmen—except the few who have to stay on duty with the campers—can socialize with the Songadeewin staff nearby.

When I was on staff, I got used to going to the dining hall for the Keewaydin Nightclub, which meant eating snacks and drinking soda, and discussing nothing much more than rapids, bears, maps, equipment, sports, a girl back home, and sometimes English literature with one of the older staffmen who was a teacher. Occasionally, we'd go off to Middlebury for a beer and, well, not much else. The only one among us who always seemed to be meeting girls on a regular basis in town was my friend John Angelo. John found the women; we found the peanut butter sandwiches.

John introduced me to an older and very sophisticated European in the foreign language school at Middlebury with eye shadow, very rare in the early 1960s. Her name was Kristen. I called her from the pay phone in the camp office, the only phone in camp. It's still the only phone in camp, by the way—cell phones don't have a prayer on Lake Dunmore—right next to the secretary's desk. Privacy was not a luxury.

Nonetheless, I successfully arranged a date. She was beautiful; she was from Scandinavia. Just her accent on the

phone already convinced me that life was treating me well.
I picked her up at her Middlebury dorm. We went to a late
dinner. I talked endlessly about camp and canoeing, trips
and hikes, and life in the woods. I think I bored her to
death, but we did drive to Blueberry Hill (yes, there was
such a place). Finally, I put my arm around her shoulder.
And then it happened. I received a tearful six-hour confes-
sional about her parents in Denmark, their divorce, her
grandparents, her brother, her boyfriend, a little more
about her boyfriend, and finally a little more about her
boyfriend. I heard it all; Ingmar Bergman had already made
the film five times. That was our date.

I got back to camp about 1:00 A.M., just as a card game
was ending in the dining hall. John Angelo saw me walking on the path to my tent.

"Are you just coming back?" he asked. I shrugged.

Back the next night at the Keewaydin Nightclub, a
bunch of us were gathered around a table in the dining
hall, talking about the upcoming celebration for Keewaydin's fiftieth anniversary. A ceremony was going to be held
at midseason, and lots of alumni would be there, including,
of course, my father, my cousins, and my uncle. Staffmen
were expected to contribute to this ceremony in some
way. Lots of ideas were bounced around that night, and at
around 1:00 A.M. we came up with the clever but edgy
concept to write a parody of the Four Winds Ceremony.

The Four Winds Ceremony is the most sacred ceremony at Keewaydin. It takes place every year, about one week into the summer, and essentially pays tribute to the mystical forces of nature, the Four Winds, (*Waban, Shawandasee, Mudjikeewis,* and *Keewaydin*) which in our version control the destiny of summer trips. I still can remember the way the ceremony fell to me the first time as an eight-year-old camper; it was haunting. How was I supposed to know that the hermit hobbling around the circle, calling the winds to attention, was actually a senior staffman? Wouldn't you have been scared if a screaming bedsheet holding a lighted torch sprinted out of nowhere into the dimly illuminated circle, put the torch to the smoldering small fire in the middle, and fired up the flame into the air? I could feel the jump in my stomach that closely followed this arrival of *Mudjikeewis,* the west wind, screaming, running, and threatening us with his painted power. This was camp theater! The winds were the characters in this play full of Native American language and lore, featuring, naturally, *Keewaydin,* the wind from the northwest, which starts in Temagami in Canada and moves south to Dunmore. To campers who would be grappling with nature a few days after the ceremony, when trips went out, it had a powerful aura, one not to be messed with.

Now years later, to us as staffmen, it seemed so right for a parody. (This year is Disneyland's fiftieth anniversary. I wonder what parody *Saturday Night Live* is thinking of doing.) As our ideas for the parody got funnier—and riskier—as the night went on, the momentum to write the parody grew. I guess in the safety of the well-lighted dining hall, with shared creativity in full force, the spirits weren't so intimidating. It was mostly younger staffmen whom I was motivating, but I seemed to be at the center of something quite risky. Forget about the spirits, I thought. What will Waboos think? What will the entire Keewaydin alumni base in the audience think? The risk of putting on this comedy that no one might find funny concerned me.

At Keewaydin, at that time in my life, I had grown by taking modest risk, from accepting the challenge to go on the Algonquin trip to driving the truck full of campers just a few summers earlier. But survival seems to be the biggest key, the biggest prerequisite, to growth. Risk is good, but survival is better. Knowing when to scale back and when not to take unnecessary risks is important.

Here, I had to weigh the risks, and I spent much of my time off a few days later alternately working on the parody of the Four Winds Ceremony and debating whether to ditch the whole idea. Something told me to go ahead with it. Returning to the nightclub, our team worked on the sketch. We worked it over and over, making it clever, smart, and risky in the right ways, we hoped.

Midseason came, and so did the alumni. The evening was dry, and the crowd of old-timers, already excited to be back at camp, was looking forward to the proceedings. Waboos began as usual with an opening song, and then, eventually, our turn arrived. A comedy was about to be presented. And after a few of our funny lines got good laughs, we relaxed and gave a great performance, which the crowd loved. To this day, Waboos talks about the day "the Four Winds Ceremony took a left turn." Looking back, it

camp

was probably the first time that I directly applied skills I had learned in the wilds of nature, at Keewaydin, to a piece of entertainment. It was my first creative challenge in front of an audience, and it is still the success I remember most fondly.

chapter fourteen

dances with wolves

present

After lunch one day a few weeks into the summer, Pepe Molina and his tent mates are sitting outside Tent 10, quietly engaging in rest hour. Rest hour in *Waramaug* has a particularly placid feel, with the lake providing a sound track of gently rippling waves. The adjacent *Waramaug* ball field, camp dining hall, and nearby camp offices are largely deserted, a dramatic change from the energetic exuberance of the rest of the day. A postlunch rest hour has been a staple of the Keewaydin schedule as far back as Waboos can remember, and for good reason. During this one part of the day, there are absolutely no decisions to be made, no obligation to decide if you want to play soccer or canoe in the lake. There's no requirement, and no reason, really, to do anything. This is a time to read or play cards or think about the past day or the future events. Soon it will be parents' weekend. Soon the summer ends for those kids at camp for four weeks, and soon new kids will arrive.

But today, about halfway into rest hour, Pepe and the boys

of Tent 10 feel restless. Tomorrow, they know, rest hour will
be sacrificed for a special event. Following lunch the *Waramaug, Wiantinaug,* and *Moosalamoo* wigwams (boys aged ten
through fifteen) will head about ninety minutes north to participate in a special Keewaydin tradition. They will attend the
dance at Brown Ledge, an all-girls camp in Colchester, Vermont, which has been a "mixing" partner with Keewaydin
for years. Every summer, the camps host an intercamp day,
highlighted by a dance, one at Brown Ledge and one at Keewaydin. On this day, the boys in Tent 10 are feeling something between excitement and apprehension.

Their emotions, even twenty-four hours in advance of
the dance, are beginning to boil over, and the boys are unable to resist the urge to begin pestering the sleeping
giant—six feet and three inches of horizontal length right
now—who lies, seemingly unconscious, ears plugged with
headphones, on a single large cot. His name is Cameron
MacDonald, and he's a nineteen-year-old sophomore at
Franklin and Marshall in Pennsylvania. He gently removes
his headphones and answers the questions that come at
him—from Pepe and from the other campers—about tomorrow's agenda. What time will they leave? How long is
the ride? What should they wear? Do they have to take
canoe paddles?

Though he's only half-awake and could dismissively
order his campers to sleep, or at least be silent, Cameron
patiently answers their questions. He talks to them, reas-
sures them, relaxes them. He knows how he revered his
own staffmen when he was in *Waramaug* a decade ago.

In 1952, my third year at the camp, my *Waramaug*

staffman was his father, Russ MacDonald, a tall Virginian in graduate school, who had been at camp for already nearly ten years, first as a camper and then on staff. Russ would go on to become a distinguished English professor at several universities, but each summer he would return to camp. For over thirty years, he was the *Waramaug* wigwam director. Russ had six sons, all of whom went to Keewaydin. Pepe's staffman, Cameron, is Russ's second-youngest son. He's spent every single summer of his life at Keewaydin.

"It's not a camp," he told me one day. "It's a way of life."

At Keewaydin, your staffman affects, shapes, and defines your summer like no other individual. Today, fifty years after my camping days, I still identify each summer by my various staffmen. It always took me two to three weeks after the end of camp to stop calling my father by the first name of my staffman for that summer. By week three, my father was no longer amused.

During my time as a camper—the 1950s—the camp still had many legendary first-generation Keewaydin staffers, many of whom were teachers and professors during the school year. There was also an influx of younger staffers, those who were making the transition from camper to staffman. Of course, no matter how old a staffman was—twenty-five, thirty-five, forty-five—he seemed, at least to me and my fellow campers, weathered and all-knowing.

Today, the mixture of younger and older staffmen remains. With older staffers remaining an active part of Keewaydin, I retain my pipe dream alive about some day going back to camp to be on staff. I have always hoped that if I changed jobs, it would be in May, so I could go to Keewaydin and work there that summer. But the only two times I did change employers were both in October. I think my wife was relieved that I couldn't wait eleven months to start a new job. She loves the camp and the impact it had on our sons, but I think her love is similar to her fondness of baseball. She's happy when her sons are on the field, but she has no interest in ever understanding the infield fly rule.

The day after that rest hour Q&A period, Pepe Molina leaves earlier than most of the campers for Brown Ledge, as he is a member of the select *Waramaug* soccer team that has been picked to represent the wigwam in a game against the Brown Ledge girls. Ahead of his fellow campers, Pepe gets a chance to survey the luxurious Brown Ledge campus, a stark contrast from the rustic simplicity of Keewaydin. Pepe walks past the log-cabin dining hall that Brown Ledge added a few years ago, and he checks out the extensive waterfront at the camp, complete with an AstroTurf-lined floating dock.

And now, as his soccer game wraps up in midafternoon, Pepe, sweat dripping down his face, knees stained with dirt, watches his fellow campers and staffmen get off the bus. Some of the boys have earnestly tried to clean up for tonight's dance, with more hair combed than usual, and the cleanest shirts that they could find in their rumpled cubbies. Perhaps most notably, Q has found an alternative to his usual white undershirt and black sweatpants ensemble, wearing a shirt that might almost be clean and a pair of shorts. Of course, there are plenty of dirty fingernails, arms and legs dotted with bites and scratches, and other symbols of a rustic summer. As the Keewaydin campers file off the bus and walk onto the pristine Brown Ledge campus, one can't help but get the image of a group of cowboys coming off a rough day on the range—and straight into a square dance.

A few minutes later, the girls and boys are sitting comfortably apart, on the grass outside Brown Ledge's equestrian course, watching the best of the Brown Ledge women show off their jumping abilities. I don't think Pepe and Q have ever even heard the word equestrian. (Horses were dropped from the Keewaydin program shortly after I left the camp in the 1960s.)

Pepe and Q seem a bit more interested in the proceedings than many of the other Keewaydin campers, some of whom have probably seen this ritual in years past. The rock music blasting through the speakers must also be odd for the Keewaydin youngsters—their camp has no speakers anywhere on the campus. The only loud music ever heard comes from cars pumping their stereos as they speed past Keewaydin Road. The stark differences between Brown Ledge and Keewaydin perhaps draw the boys closer together, at least for now, as the dance looms on the horizon. As Waboos says, Keewaydin creates lots of challenges for the boys, but this challenge—girls—is not one that the camp tends to push. Except tonight.

Observing the *Waramaug* campers during the hour of free time that follows the equestrian display is quite telling. The girls are comfortable and at home on their campus, wandering from cabin to cabin in small packs. Predictably, a few of the older *Moosalamoo* campers remember the "friends" they made at Brown Ledge the previous summer, and groups of the teenagers socialize in the grass. The young *Waramaug*ers, though, have no such experience on this turf. They trail their staffmen to resting spots and form small circles of conversation. The staffmen share stories of when they first came to Brown Ledge. The Keewaydin staff is on full alert, watching out for the campers in this foreign situation and making them as comfortable as possible.

By the time dinner comes around, every *Waramaug*er is accounted for by a staffman. The meal is an elaborate buffet, with sandwich meats, salad, fresh fruit, and more. Once again, the younger girls and boys remain virtually separate, with no mixing yet.

When dinner is over, down the wood-chip path everyone goes to the dance, which is being held in the camp's playhouse, complete with built-in bleacher seats and a stage. The area in front of the stage, surrounded by the steep bleachers, is quickly commandeered by the older kids, and the younger *Waramaug*ers find themselves on the stage.

Soon, a few campers have matched up and are clumsily but happily dancing. A few others follow suit, and it's not long before the camps have mixed. Standing in the middle of the stage, Pepe feels a tap on his shoulder. It's a boy from his tent, telling him that a girl "over there" wants to dance with him. Despite his boasts to other campers earlier in the day that he wouldn't do anything of the sort, Pepe eagerly agrees and is soon bending his knees to the music with a young girl who is about his size. Over his shoulder, Q is mixing with another group of girls and will soon be coyly dancing in a group with some friends and a few Brown Ledge campers.

The Brown Ledge dance started as an exercise in wallflower growth; now it's a smashing success.

The bus ride home from Brown Ledge is electric with buzz. Campers joyfully exchange fish tales from the night—"I danced with six girls!" "I danced with five!" "I danced with one girl the whole night!"—as they bask in the collective joy of a great day. One boy, Will, recalls the last girl he danced with. He notes sheepishly to his staffman on the seat across the aisle, "The name Jennie is nice, don't you think?" The staffer, a twenty-three-year-old, laughs knowingly! In the rear of the bus, Q is already fast asleep, another new experience behind him. He's probably already dreaming about playing basketball tomorrow during free time, imagining some innovations on his spin move. Pepe is soon asleep as well. He met several girls who were smitten by his wide grin, and the last one he shared a dance with bent down and boldly kissed him good night on the cheek.

The campers sleepwalk from the bus to their tents, many out cold even before their heads hit their pillows. About a half-hour later, the dining hall light goes on, and the staffmen meet for Nightclub. All the talk is about the dance, and the *Waramaug* staffmen gather at a table off to the side to laugh about the campers they saw dancing awkwardly a few hours ago. This kid said he got a phone number, and that kid was dancing with a girl two feet taller than he is!

Waboos walks in with Russ MacDonald, who sits him at a table in the center and fetches him a cup of tea. Waboos is talking about the new campers that will arrive soon. A staffman walks up to Waboos, identifies himself, and sits down. Waboos asks how the dance went this year. The staffman tells him it was just fine. Waboos nods and goes back to talking about the four-week changeover at midseason. Everything is back to normal on Lake Dunmore.

chapter fifteen

breck's first day

1979

Are there moments in life where joy and anxiety and fear and uncontrollable emotions take over to the point that your skin color actually changes and your stomach seems to reside in your throat?

There are. And I'm convinced they usually involve your children.

I was so calm, so cool, so together when my eldest son, Breck, was born in 1970. Yes, he was a little slow to come into the world. Yes, his umbilical cord was wrapped around his neck. Yes, I was ushered out of the delivery room at New York Hospital. Yet I was still rational and almost confident. When I went into Jane's room an hour after the birth and the nurse in pink brought little yellow Breck into the room, I looked at him, turned to Jane, back to him, and began to cry. I couldn't remember the last time I'd cried.

Nine years later, Jane, Breck, Eric, and I set off from Los Angeles to my parents' home in Saxton's River, Vermont. We were going to spend the weekend with my father and mother before taking Breck for his first night at Keewaydin. Breck knew all about the camp. He knew I went there and his grandfather went there and all the rest of the family's history there. My sister—his aunt—had gone to Songadeewin. He had heard me hum camp songs, heard me talk about Waboos, heard about my adventures in the *Annwi* wigwam as an eight-year-old.

During our time at the farm, my father seemed to make it a special point to tell stories about his adventures at Keewaydin. My father walked with Breck in the woods to describe the Vermont topography. Breck just stared at him. Five-year-old Eric, tagging along, was interested in how plants were similar to people. "Don't they have bones, too, so they can stand up?" he asked.

They got home, and my father told all of us that he thought Breck had a great time even though he hadn't said much. Then my father got out the maps and boxes of camp memorabilia to continue his tutorial on the camp. Breck continued to stare silently at him.

The next morning, my mother and Jane took Breck to Sam's Army and Navy Store in Bellows Falls for last-minute supplies—bug oil, a Boy Scout knife, a few comic books. Later, back at home, my father read Breck and Eric stories about camping, but Eric seemed more interested in the stories than his eight-year-old brother. Breck was clearly fearful about going to camp, and it was up to me to sit with him, to calm him. I tried, telling him about the bathrooms—well, forts—and the showers he was going to take and how that wasn't so bad. I told him the trips were short. I told him that his grandparents were only two hours away, even though his parents were three thousand miles away. I told him the staff was friendly and the kids were nice. I told him it wasn't school.

My reassurances were dishonest. I was scared to death for him. I had to hide it all; I had to act confident and express delight in the fun he was going to have. This was the first time I realized that your children's fear is worse than your own fear. It was like dealing with your child before he could talk and knowing he felt sick.

Sitting on the bed in my parents' house, Breck suddenly piped up.

"Who is going to cut my toenails?" he asked me. I was stumped. It was the same kind of question as "Where do I go when I die?"—the kind that I usually left up to his mother to answer. I heard Eric, still happily chatting with his grandparents downstairs, without a clue to the world's troubles. I was envious of him.

The next day, we headed toward camp, two hours away, with a stop at McDonald's in Rutland for one last shot at civilization. On the way, I sang every camp song I knew, and I knew a lot. My wife thought my performance was odd at best. We drove through Brandon and up the back road on Route 53 to camp. Breck said from the back that he was scared. I said everything would be great. Breck said he didn't want to go. I said it would be the best time of his life; at that moment, I wished I could take him home.

Breck asked me for the telephone number at my

parents' house. I couldn't tell him there were no phones at camp. I gave him my parents' number anyway.

We arrived at camp and walked around, heading for *Annwi,* the youngest wigwam. It had been about fifteen years since I'd been at the camp, but I knew every inch of the place, almost every pebble. And I knew a lot of people. Waboos came right up to me in his familiar duck waddle, yelling out, "Hi, Mike. How's your dad, and your uncle, and John Angelo?" Breck had never heard anybody call me anything but Michael. He knew this was a special relationship from the past, just as I had when I heard Waboos call my father Les.

We arrived at his wigwam, met his staffman, and started unpacking. "Breck, do you want to try to pass your twenty-five-yard swim test?" his staffman asked, perhaps sensing his anxiety. Or maybe it was our anxiousness, despite the fact we had practiced this swim repeatedly in California.

"Okay," he answered, and off he went with two other kids. His mother continued unpacking while Eric and I watched from the dock.

A few minutes later, he returned from the water; he had passed.

"Congratulations," I said, but before he could answer, he was talking to another kid, who had also passed.

We finished unpacking. "Breck, we can stay a couple more hours," I said, but he stopped me short and said, "That's okay, I'm fine." And he ran off with that other kid.

Twenty minutes later, after walking around a bit more and chatting with Waboos, I went with Eric and Jane to tell

camp

Breck we had to leave. All four of us walked to the car. I tried to figure out how I would say good-bye. I recalled my mother telling me about the conversation I had with her when I was fourteen and she left me at prep school. She told me that as she and my father left after driving me down to Lawrenceville, New Jersey, I had said, "It's okay. You go. I'll just sit on the bed and think for a few hours." My mother said it took them months to get over that image.

There we were at the car, and all Breck wanted to do was get back to his tent, or so he said. We hugged and kissed while Eric threw rocks in the lake. We hugged again and got in the car. As we yelled good-bye and headed down the driveway toward the camp exit, Breck didn't move. He didn't run back to the tent like he said he was going to. He just stood there.

"We have to stop," I said. Jane said it would be best to just keep going.

There he was, in my rearview mirror, staring at us.

"We can't leave. Look at him." I realized I hadn't taken my foot off the accelerator. "Okay, you're right, he's okay." And we drove out in silence. I looked over.

Tears were rolling down Jane's face. I kept my eyes on the road.

chapter sixteen

indian circle

present

The summer always seems to go by more quickly at Keewaydin when you find yourself measuring the time by the
passing of weekly events—the Thursday-night barbecues,
Friday Frolics, and Sunday Circles (nondenominational), to
name a few. When you think, "Wow, another week went by
already," all the great moments and memories of the seven
days seem to telescope into one swift event. Then again,
maybe time does simply fly faster on the shores of Lake
Dunmore.

One of Keewaydin's weekly gathering traditions actually serves to commemorate all the great events of the past
week and is intended to slow the summer down, forcing
the campers to recall and recount their best experiences.
This is the campwide Sunday-evening campfire, where
The Kicker is read and where stories are told, held at the
Wiantinaug Indian Circle. This Indian Circle, which sits
right on the lake, is probably the most aesthetically pleas-
ing of all the campfire areas, and campwide events have

been held there for generations. In addition to the normal circular smattering of wooden benches around a campfire, there is a wooden post on the edge of the circle adjacent to the lake, where the leaders of any gathering sit. On the post is a plaque with the names and years of the five Keewaydin directors who have come and gone. Peter Hare, the current director, has not yet posted his name above his father's.

And tonight, as he has since 1923, in some capacity or another, Waboos sits with the rest of Keewaydin at the campfire and listens to stories being read about the baseball game in *Waramaug,* the first trip for several *Annwi* campers to Greenhill Point, the preparations in *Moosalamoo* for the big three-week trip up the Algonquin. In between the readings, a variety of festivities intercede—a staffman juggles, songs are sung. It's a rhythm familiar to me—I used to love writing for and participating in the Sunday *Kicker*—and a rhythm familiar to Waboos.

Waboos, of course, sees only in blurs, but you wonder if he can see what I see at the circle, the one thing that is different at the Sunday Circle from years ago. The faces have changed: their colors, their complexions, their designs. There are white kids, black kids, Asian kids, Latino kids, all collected around this campfire in Vermont. Some are from far-off states (and, in a few cases, nations) and represent ethnicities and backgrounds not present at Keewaydin years ago. Further, some are on scholarship, an opportunity offered to families without resources of their own to provide for an experience at camp.

Here, diversity for the future is meshing with tradition.

camp

The Sunday campfire is slowing. No new logs have been added for forty-five minutes, so that the embers barely illuminate the tired eyes of the campers as the evening gets closer to its conclusion. At this moment, Peter Hare paces in front of what is left of the fire, with Waboos seated and barely visible behind one shoulder. Pete paces, in part, because his legs are so stiff; not only has he been sitting like everyone else for the last two hours, but earlier today, he endured a ten-hour car ride. He paces also because he's a bit anxious; he wants to find the right words at this moment, stemming from the journey he has just taken. In his right hand, he grips a canteen of water like a trophy he has brought back from a distant shore. He paces because this is one of those sacred moments at camp where past, present, and future will intertwine.

About two hours ago, before everyone filed into the Indian Circle, Waboos was brought ahead of the camper rush by his daughter, Laurie. By the time the campers arrived, he'd been sitting for a few moments in a big wooden chair reserved for him, ensconced like a beloved monarch on his throne before the rest of the court filled in. Tonight, he is bundled up to prepare for the dropping temperatures, wearing his standard Dickies khaki pants and brown boat shoes, with two sweaters thrown on top of his trademark polo shirt.

Every day this summer, he's worn these pants; I guess only a few of his family members know whether he actually has more than one pair. The shirts are all old, some probably older than my children, but he alternates these, a different color at least every other day. On the outside of this ensemble tonight is an ancient wool cardigan sweater adorned with a giant P, in Penn colors, his alma mater. You get the feeling he might have gotten the sweater as a graduation gift—over sixty-five years ago. The weathered nature of his wardrobe seems at this point to be a testament to his own ageless aura, almost suggesting to the observer that he hasn't left camp once in the past eighty-one years to buy clothes, because they hardly matter.

In the 1970s, after Waboos retired from teaching at the Montgomery School, he, as one might expect, immersed himself even more in camp activities. He also became more active in the national summer-camping scene, serving a term as president of his section of the American Camping Association. While his partners, Slim and Abby, had by this time found other interests besides their investment—financial and emotional—in Keewaydin, Waboos remained committed full-time. With the economy suffering, camp enrollment was down, and help was needed to try to fill the wigwam rosters each summer. Private donations also took a hit, including the General Breed Scholarship Fund, named after the old director, which had provided financial assistance to families who wanted to send their kids to Keewaydin but couldn't afford the tuition on their own. With such support now diminished, the camp's growth suffered for a few years, and as the end of the 1970s approached—while Waboos, Abby, and Slim continued to age—they began to think about ways not only to ensure that the camp would survive past their time as leaders but also to find a way to ensure strong support for the General Breed Fund.

It was on a Memorial Day weekend cleanup when the next great idea was born. Some veteran staffers had returned before the summer to clean up the camp in preparation for the arriving campers. Over the course of the weekend, Waboos and Abby mentioned to a group of the staffers the dilemma of perpetuating Keewaydin. Ideas continued to get tossed around, and some of the alumni—parents and friends of these staffers—became involved. A few years later, Waboos, Abby, and Slim sold Keewaydin to a newly formed group called the Keewaydin Foundation, which would provide perpetual ownership for the camp and ensure that its mission and direction remained the same as it had for the previous century.

Waboos would remain on board as director, while the foundation—a group of men who idolized him and what he had done for their camp—handled the finances, fundraising, and future growth. After a dicey few years, the camp flourished, and it is currently in better shape than ever.

While Keewaydin is immersed in the eternal rituals of the Sunday campfire and *The Kicker*, on the other side of Lake Dunmore, about a fifteen-minute canoe paddle away, another camp meets in similar fashion, campers sitting in a giant circle on the banks of the water. It's the same drill:

Campers and staff laugh and reminisce about the week that has just passed. Waboos's grandchildren are in the circle, and the camp is run by a former director of the *Annwi* wigwam at Keewaydin. Lots of similarities, with one striking difference: Everyone in the circle is female.

The original Songadeewin, meaning "strong of heart" in Algonquin, was started years ago at Lake Willoughby in Vermont, nearly 150 miles northeast of Lake Dunmore. The camp was a great success in its early years, the 1920s, and even after the Keewaydin camps split up in the 1930s, but ultimately it closed in 1975. As the newly formed Keewaydin Foundation gained support from alumni and families throughout the 1980s, one of the ideas for expansion was to find a place to reopen Songadeewin. Sure enough, when nearby Camp Dunmore closed down a few years ago, the owners were happy to sell the land to Keewaydin to ensure that young kids would continue to spend summers there, and Songadeewin was reopened in 1999 on the other side of the lake.

Sitting next to each other in the Songadeewin Indian Circle tonight are Noelle and Veronica, who came along on the daunting journey with Pepe and Q nearly four weeks ago from the San Fernando Valley. They are both incredibly sharp young women, and, as girls tend to be in their pre-teen years, more assertive than Pepe and Q. At the beginning of the summer, while we stood in the parking lot of the Middlebury Inn getting set to head to camp, I recall Noelle, a great reader and writer, talking about school and telling me that she "abhors math." Abhors?

Sitting amid the other hundred campers, Noelle and

Veronica can look across and see Ellen Flight, Songadeewin's founding director. Ellen is a Keewaydin lifer; her father, Dave, was in Waboos's eighth-grade math class at the Montgomery School, and he became a longtime staffman at Keewaydin. He was the guy who never finished that World War II story he was reading to us when I was in *Annwi* in 1950.

Ellen followed her father through Keewaydin and eventually became *Annwi* director, her passion and skill overcoming the fact that she hadn't been a Keewaydin camper. Thanks to a familiarity with the Keewaydin program, Ellen had no qualms about incorporating the general Keewaydin schedule into Songadeewin's—especially the traditions of tripping and canoeing. Like Pepe and Q, Noelle's and Veronica's trips this summer have been among their best experiences.

Still, a closer glance at Songa—as the girls call it—reveals that while the camp is a testament to the enduring universality of Keewaydin ideals, it also is a living example of how the camp has adapted those ideals to fit an all-girls environment. The camp has a smartly progressive and original program, one designed to do all the things that Keewaydin does for campers—improve their abilities of self-confidence, initiative, teamwork—but do it in a way that is mindful that the lessons are being absorbed by young women.

"I think the thing we work the hardest on is to have the girls feel confident and strong about standing up and speaking their mind," says Ellen Flight. "We spend a lot of time deliberately getting kids up to speak in front of the group." They do say "Help the other fellow" at Songa, but first and foremost, the mantra of this camp is "Strong of

Heart," encouraging the girls to grow confident and self-assured about themselves. At Keewaydin, while this is a main goal, it is not buttressed by a slogan.

"I got a letter last fall from a guy who was at Keeway-din for years," Ellen told me. "He had his daughter come here, and he was like, 'What is that Strong of Heart thing?' At the end of the summer, he wrote me a letter and said, 'I understand much better what Strong of Heart is now. I get it.'"

This Strong of Heart spirit is what persuaded Noelle and Veronica to volunteer to host a show that will be held at Songa in a few days—in front of the whole camp. They have prepared a routine and have been practicing it all week. Something tells me they will be great.

Following the rebirth of Songadeewin, the Keewaydin Foundation reached its pinnacle in 2001, with the announcement that it had completed a purchase that had been in the works for the better part of a decade. Several hundred miles north, the original Keewaydin, on an island in Lake Temagami in Ontario, had been surviving for decades after the camps had been split up in the 1930s. But enrollment there had steadily dropped to perilously small numbers; Temagami is deep in the Canadian wilderness, and tripping is its sole activity. Reuniting became a life preserver for Temagami, a perfect mission for the Keeway-din Foundation, and an important symbolic repartnering for both camps.

camp

Back across the lake, Peter Hare is standing in front of the campfire, his pacing slowed a bit as he begins his talk to the campers and staff. It hasn't been the easiest of seasons for him, his first as director of Keewaydin *and* executive director of the foundation. Pulling double duty meant lots of long nights this winter at the camp office, about twenty minutes from his house in Middlebury.

He feels reinvigorated as he stands in front of the group, ready to tell them about his amazing journey to Camp Keewaydin Temagami to see how the aging older brother is doing. He tells them about the camp you can only get to by boat, and the beautiful lake, uninhabited and undisturbed. No cars drive by on any nearby roads, and you don't have to close your eyes to imagine what the place was like a hundred years ago—because it's still as primitive as it was then.

Peter tells them all this, and then holds up a canteen that he filled early this morning with water from Lake Temagami. He smiles and sheepishly notes that the jug was originally full but is now half-empty, since he got thirsty on the drive back. He offers a trivia question: He asks the campers to tell him how Keewaydin Temagami and Keewaydin Dunmore originally split up, and why. Dozens of hands shoot up, with a chorus of "Ooh, ooh, me, me" pleadings. Peter eventually calls on a *Waramaug* camper named Charlie from Tent 5. Charlie, true to form, recites the history correctly.

"Now, Charlie," Peter says, "I want you to come up here, please. It's time for you to symbolically unite our two camps."

Charlie takes the jug of water from Peter, who whispers more instructions into his ear, and walks carefully over to the dock behind the Indian Circle. The campers and staff stand to get a better look, but it's dark over by the water, and they can hear only his movements. Keewaydin is silent; only the faint crackling of the fire and the hiss of a soft breeze can be heard.

Charlie opens the jug, and the water slowly pours from Lake Temagami into Lake Dunmore.

chapter seventeen

visiting day

1983

When I was a camper, midseason at camp was filled with excitement because it was parents' weekend. Surprisingly, I found, it didn't even compare to the rising anticipation for me as a parent. So one summer in the 1980s, with Breck already a veteran at Keewaydin and Eric in his first year, I spent the week before visiting day somewhat distracted and excited.

After this week of buildup, we—Jane, our youngest son, Anders, and I—took a flight to Hartford (through Chicago), rented a van, and drove off to the familiar checkpoint, my parents' house in southern Vermont. We would be spending a day there, and then taking them along to camp the next day. That summer, we were traveling with another couple from California, the singer and songwriter Neil Diamond and his wife, Marcia, who were going to visit their son, a close friend of my son Breck.

That year was particularly important because Eric—redheaded and left-handed, a genetic replica of his mother—had gotten off to a shaky start in *Annwi*. While

Breck had been dubious from the instant we had arrived, Eric had been the opposite—seemingly not nervous at all when we dropped him off in June before going to visit Jane's parents in Jamestown, New York. But a few days later, while we were relaxing in the backyard there, a letter arrived from him to his grandparents. "Dear Grandma and Grandpa, If my parents are there, send them back here to pick me up." The next day, another letter arrived, addressed to us, and forwarded from our home in California.

Dear Mom and Dad,
I want you to go back to Jamestown because I whant [*sic*] to leave in a few days. Hope things are better there then they are here. I am a worse [this] time then [*sic*] the first few days. I have been telling Ken [his staffman] and Breck, they are trying to help me. I am getting home sick [*sic*] as much. I have done a lot of activities.
Love Eric

Needless to say, we were concerned. Back home in California, another letter soon followed. "Dear Mom and Dad, Camp is ok but I am only staying one month [he was scheduled for two] and I am not going on any trips." To me, the optimist, maybe things were sounding better, but Jane still felt we had sent him to Siberia. Then:

Dear Mom and Dad,
I am having a pretty good time, not a great time. I am getting home sick [*sic*] a lot. It is boring at most parts. I want to go home at midseason. Please send candy.

Someone took all of my candy. I don't like the people in my cabin. We are doing good in inspection.
Love, Eric.

A more reassuring letter came from Ken, his staffman, who said Eric was doing fine and seemed to be adjusting well. We called, and I explained the situation to Waboos, who was not surprised. "This happens often—not to worry," he told me. I listened to him and decided not to worry . . . for a few days. Now, as I rode the last leg in the car from Connecticut to Vermont, I was definitely worrying again.

One of several entrepreneurial enterprises my father embarked upon was starting an apple business in Vermont. It wasn't a great financial opportunity, but he always seemed happy up there, in the state where he had spent the most formative days of his youth. He would be up each weekend morning at 6:00 A.M., mending walls, clearing fields, planting trees. He spent the rest of his time during the workweek being a lawyer and entrepreneur, and making my mother feel at home in the city.

After a long day of traveling and adjusting to the time change, we were finally in Vermont, the Diamonds and ourselves, heading to the orchard, something I'd done hundreds of times, coming back to visit my parents, now with my children. Coming home, even as an adult, created a mixture of emotions, 95 percent positive but 5 percent tinged with memories of adolescent conflict, of being grounded, of the pressures to get good grades in school, of sibling tattletales, and of all those other episodes that are part of growing up.

We drove straight to my sister's orchard house, which is about a mile from my parents' house and which I had helped renovate with my father. We would see my parents in the morning. On the way, we saw a discarded old van turned over on its side next to the road. Swastikas were painted all over the vehicle, along with a message: "Kill the Jews that Hitler missed!" Even odder was the fact that it was signed in big red letters with the name of a troubled young man living down the road, who years earlier had worked for my father pruning apple trees.

Marcia and Jane expressed their dismay and anger. Neil sat silently. We drove to the house without talking and called my father. He was incredulous, hopping in his car and speeding down the mile-long road to the orchard house. My mother stayed at their house, manning the phone, prepared to call the police. Later, we all sat in my sister's kitchen and talked nearly all night.

The next morning, walking to my parents' house, trying to clear our heads, knowing we were going to walk past the painted van, we crossed paths with our neighbors, the Kibbys. Mr. Kibby had worked in the post office in Saxton's River for years. I didn't really want to have a conversation about the graffiti on the overturned vehicle. It was too awkward. I had become the outsider, and in spite of my own feelings of outrage, I was embarrassed. As we grew closer, we saw that Sue and Mrs. Kibby had just fin-

ished painting over the offensive insults. The spray paint-
ings were gone. I was surprised by such a generous act. I
tried to thank them.

"This is disgusting" is all they said as they kept walking,
headed for home. Suddenly, the van was lying there like a
heap on the road, now a meaningless piece of junk. And we
were calmed, even though the state police still showed up.
Later in the day, Neil and I found some humor in how he
was living a real-life version of *The Jazz Singer*, a film he
had recently made. Two weeks later, a local Vermont judge
sentenced the perpetrator to some "thinking time" in jail,
saying, "I fought in World War II to stop this type of
behavior."

Back at the house, it was time to focus again on my
kids, the weekend's original agenda. My mother served
lunch at the pond for all of us; Anders played with tadpoles
and tried to swim in the frigid water. I grilled fat cheese-
burgers and Vermont corn. My father told stories—mostly
to Anders—about sports and horses and, of course, camp.
Anders kept up the questions, reminding me of my own
tendency to ask, ask, ask. My father had great patience for
his youngest grandson, and he kept answering.

To his credit, my father was a very good athlete. When
the conversation moved on to swimming that afternoon,
he dived—both to cool off and to show off—into the very
cold pond, turning a somersault off the dock. It was im-
pressive, at least until he emerged quickly, shaking off water
almost like a dog. Something seemed odd. After a few
moments, I saw him whispering to my mother, and then
saying, louder, that something was wrong. He was pointing

to his heart and feeling his pulse, then grabbing his chest, sitting down, lying down, turning white. My son was oblivious to his reaction, having found a frog in the pond.

I sprang into action, for the first time in my life ordering my father to stay still, a new kind of reversal of responsibilities. I ran down to the orchard house to get our pickup truck. I drove my father to the hospital in Hanover, New Hampshire, an hour north. All of a sudden, the great athlete was an older man in trouble, a scared older man. Ironically, I wasn't the panicked son. I didn't have time to be, I guess.

By late the next morning, things were almost back to normal—or at least on the way there. After an overnight medicinal drip to stop his arrhythmia, my father was resting. Jane and my mother were on their way to the hospital to pick him up. They would take him to camp and meet me there; I was headed straight to visiting day with everyone else.

I found Eric sitting in *Annwi* at the wigwam's Indian Circle. He smiled and gave a little wave as I made my way over. "Camp is great. It's cool. It's fun. Have you seen Breck yet?" Then: "Where's Mom?" There wasn't one mention of being unhappy. Then he was off to canoeing, to prepare for the midseason demonstration of mastery in the water—where campers show off newly acquired skills like turning, stroking, and poling (propelling upstream) the canoe in a variety of different ways. After I wandered around a bit and found Breck, Jane arrived with my parents. My father was walking around defiantly, unfazed by the outcome of his bravado the day before.

A few hours later, as I ate a few more camp burgers grilled on *Waramaug* ball field and found myself finally almost relaxing, I caught a glimpse of my sons—all three, all without life jackets, including young Anders—getting into a sailboat near the waterfront. My father—only hours after his heart scare—was getting in with them and pushing off from the dock. Noting the strong breeze, with the boat sailing on its edge, on the brink of turning over, I began waving frantically at them, concerned for their safety. I had reverted to being eclipsed by a bigger-than-life father, at least in my mind. After they returned to shore safely, I said nothing, even though I was angry at my father for ignoring the danger to my kids. I watched silently as he enjoyed his moment as the triumphant grandfather. I did what I always did when my father annoyed me. I complained to my mother, who did what she always did (such are family dynamics)—refer me back to my wife.

Soon afterward, there was my father in the annual parade of old-timers, proudly striding alongside Waboos as the participants marched in chronological sequence, according to their years at Keewaydin. Watching this, all I could think about was this camp's history, my father's intense feelings for the camp, his incredible pride in all the generations of Eisners who had gone to Keewaydin . . . his intense feelings, which had embarrassed me at times.

And then I realized Jane was looking at me and probably thinking the same things—about me.

chapter eighteen

good night,
keewaydin, good night

present

Even at the outset of a hot and sunny summer day, the early morning at Keewaydin is cool and damp. A low cloud of steam rises off the lake, hovering like a layer of wet dust, and the grass is moist with dew, a soggy green carpet.

To an outsider up and at 'em before the first gong is sounded at 7:30, the Keewaydin campus has an odd aura of expectation, like an empty stadium before a big game. The flaps of all the tents are pulled down, keeping the cold air out. The fields and pathways are quiet, almost vacant, with only occasional movement from those whose days have already begun. Peter Hare, in a teal windbreaker and rubber hiking boots, glides across *Waramaug* ball field to his office to get a few minutes of work done before breakfast. His gait is clean and efficient, his feet barely leaving the ground as he moves. Before he was slowed by arthritic hips and falling eyesight, Waboos, too, moved this way.

Inside the office, Peter isn't alone. A few staffers have

been inside for some time; it's one of the few times of the day when they can get work done without being interrupted by staffmen and campers. Nearby, inside the dining hall, one can hear the loud groans of chairs moving along the floor and the muted clangs of plates as the staff sets up for breakfast. Over by the *Waramaug* tents, the flaps are drawn open, and small figures poke out, about one per minute. They scurry off to the fort, then scamper back to their tents and huddle underneath their blankets, looking to grab a few more precious seconds of sleep.

Charmed by the playful innocence of this dashing and darting, one might miss a familiar figure slowly making his way across the field. Years ago, Waboos would have been the first one across the campus, arriving in his office early. Now he has happily ceded that role to his son. Yet he still eagerly awaits the beating of the gong in the morning, hearing and feeling Keewaydin awakening.

Now comes a crescendo of action, culminating in the ascent of the youngsters up the steps of the dining hall. On some mornings, Waboos will head to his cottage, Hare House, to sit at his desk, waiting to be picked up by a friend, or a son or daughter, and taken to Table 1. Other mornings, like this one, he'll just stand at the side of the field, greeting campers and staff, welcoming them to the glorious New England day. As always, he sets the tone with his refusal to complain at what the aging process has wrought.

Coming to breakfast, Pepe and Q know this is a very special morning. Today is visiting day, the final day of the first session of camp; their mothers, after a cross-country journey identical to the one that their boys had taken a month ago, will be on campus shortly.

A month has gone by, and their summer is nearly complete. Two lives shaped by Keewaydin have just started.

An hour later, as they skip out of the dining hall to morning formation, Pepe and Q stand out this morning, even more than their fellow campers, for their giddiness and goofiness. The postbreakfast hour flies by. Staffmen urge campers to clean up for a special visiting-day inspection, but that idea dissolves when eager families staying at nearby inns and motels begin to flood into Keewaydin. Pepe's and Q's mother stayed last night at the Middlebury Inn, and they are in the first wave of parents to arrive.

Pepe runs and greets his mother with a giant hug (for such a small boy), while Q, always the cool cat, is a bit less animated with his affection. This isn't surprising: Pepe has been talking about his mother all summer, telling his staffman Cameron how much she means to him, how wonderful she is, and how much he misses her. For Q, never the overly emotional sort, his latent enthusiasm is expected.

Pepe, in Spanish chatter that's even faster than his English, unleashes a torrent of words, telling his mother everything about camp. The commentary is accompanied by fingers gesturing in various directions—the basketball court, the baseball field, the lake, the dining hall, the fort.

Pepe's mom takes it all in, quiet and shy, sticking close to her son. She is—like her son four weeks ago—very far from the familiar. Now they are in Tent 5, sitting on Pepe's cot as he shows her keepsakes from the summer, everything from his flashlight to his Keewaydin T-shirt. He continues to hold her hand as he tries to describe everything he's done since he left Orange County a month ago.

In his less demonstrative way, Q gives his mother a tour of his life since he came east, as well. Q's mom immediately begins needling her son about his messy cubby and dirty clothes. After some initial coddling, Q prepares to go about his business, with his mother more at arm's length. He locates his life preserver to get ready for the upcoming canoe races scheduled for the last day. Nonetheless, he continues to throw glances back at his mother to make sure she is watching.

In their own unique ways, Pepe and Q are showing off—sure, they're thrilled and comforted by the sight of their moms, but, more significantly, they're set on showing them how much they've learned, what they've accomplished, and what their life is like at Keewaydin; that they've survived and thrived in this new world. They're trying to see if in just a day their moms can grasp why the journey was worth it.

All over campus, the day takes on a circuslike quality. Cars are double-parked in the lots across Keewaydin Road. Parents, grandparents, aunts and uncles, sisters and brothers, older and younger—they all have descended on Keewaydin.

By tradition, this last morning is devoted to canoeing, the heart of the camp's heritage. Boys in all wigwams assemble in assigned teams for the annual end-of-the-session series of races in Keewaydin's historic—but still in pristine mint condition—wooden canoes. Some of the canoes are as much as five decades old, and others are newer, built by one of America's greatest canoe craftsmen, Keewaydin alumnus Schuyler Thomson. Ojibway style birchbark canoes that were originally used at Keewaydin Temagami have given way to these streamlined canoes, which are painted a rich forest green and inscribed with dedications to past campers on their bases. Scanning the boats—as campers can be seen doing from time to time—is a lesson in Keewaydin history: You'll see four Hares, three MacDonalds, a few Flights, and other familiar names.

The races are an exhibition of controlled havoc, with staffmen in the water getting the canoes set and marking their start as the boats race about seventy-five yards parallel to the shore. There are solo races, doubles (two campers in each canoe), and quads, or those famous (or infamous) "mojos" (four in each canoe). There are no medal ceremonies or proclamations honoring the victors; if anything, the main challenge after each race is to try to figure out who won. Since there are no microphones or sound systems at the camp, there is no way to make announcements. After each race, the campers waddle out of the water and carefully place their canoes back in the appropriate storage rack. All the parents want to do at this point is congratulate their kids on making it safely back to shore.

It's hard for parents to make out their own kids in the canoes, especially tiny Pepe. The smaller campers race against one another, and the same goes for the bigger campers. Q's mother has brought her bathing suit, and, shoes off, she ambles with a camera ankle-deep into the water of Lake Dunmore to see if she can locate her son's boat.

After the canoe races, the day reverts to a largely normal schedule, so parents can watch their kids in action at camp. After morning activities and a buffet lunch comes rest hour. While some parents—including those of Pepe and Q—sneak their kids off for a trip to Ben & Jerry's or the A&W, other families can't resist spreading out by the tents and relaxing alongside their sons, happy with the opportunity to take an hour off themselves.

As rest hour ends and afternoon activity commences, families fill Waboos's cottage. There are former campers and staffmen reminiscing with their old mentor and boss, wives and mothers itching to catch more than a glimpse of this leader with the strange name they have heard about for so long, brothers and sisters dragged in, suddenly entranced by the wall of pictures that seems to tell its own story, and the ageless man who presides here. Standing nearby, Russ MacDonald and Laurie Hare are suddenly just nobles in the court, diversions for those who wait their turn to talk to Waboos.

The visitors ask about the summer, how everything has been going. Those who have known Waboos over the years anticipate that his answer will focus on how great a time the campers have been having, how the weather cooperated for the trips, what a nice job the staff is doing. Everything is positive with Waboos. He won't hint that his wife, Katie, is sicker than most know; won't admit, even to himself, that he is in pain from this, that there can be life and death in the world outside Keewaydin. Nobody dares ask why she hasn't been there for a few summers.

Waboos's daughter now stands at his side, talking to some parents about their sons' projects, which she supervised in arts and crafts this summer. His son Peter is outside on *Waramaug* ball field, charming parents as Waboos did for so many summers, telling them things they never knew about their own children.

Back outside, by the lake, the afternoon activities have begun. Pepe's baseball team is playing in this final game of the session, between the so-called South and West units, while Q's North team is the odd squad out. In trademark fashion, Q knows exactly what he wants to do, and he puts his life preserver back on and heads to the lake. After mastering a variety of activities and sports at camp—basketball, mountain climbing, canoeing, diving, boxing—in the last week, he's suddenly been entranced with kayaking, and he

michael d. eisner

has become a regular at staffman Bo Saxby's lessons. With no more than four campers ever showing up for the activity, and an engaged teacher like Bo, Q has picked up the skills quickly. While his mother stands knee-deep in Lake Dunmore, camera continuing to flash, Q does his single rolls (yes, it's just what it sounds like—actually rolling the kayak, and the camper inside, 360 degrees).

About thirty feet away, perched on some large rocks behind the backstop, Pepe's mom sits as her son claps his mitt in left field. As colorful and emotional as Pepe usually is, he seems a bit more reserved since lunch. Sure, he's still his combative and playful self, joking with staffmen, but with each of his signature moves, Pepe looks back at his mother. While Q's mom makes small talk with some parents and suns herself in the glistening light off the lake, Pepe's mom remains away from the action. Pepe, the dutiful son, returns to her side each inning, the two huddled close together, whispering.

Then, suddenly, he is gone. When Pepe's turn at bat comes up in the third inning, he is nowhere to be seen. It's not a major problem; with thirteen campers in the lineup, the game continues with little disruption. Where is Pepe? A likely spot: inside his tent, on his bed, opposite his mother, as the two struggle to zip his duffel bag closed. She reminded him they needed to finish packing, and they went back to the tent to do just that. His mother is clearly a stranger to the traditions of Keewaydin, where campers can have fun now and pack later.

Pepe is happy to see his mother, just like the scores of other campers who right now share the joys of camp with their families. Fathers share canoes with sons; mothers and sisters play tennis opposite male counterparts; older brothers stand impressed on the basketball court, watching siblings who are better shooters than they were a month ago. One hopes that by the end of visiting day, by tonight, Pepe and his mother can find something to bond over at camp besides packing to leave. Maybe the distance between the two worlds, between the two cultures, is simply too great—at least too great a distance to make up in a single day.

Nightfall can sneak up on you at Keewaydin, as it has on the scores of parents who continue to swarm the *Waramaug* campus. Pepe and Q are nearly all packed. Bags and trunks are loaded into cars, and somehow upon final sweeps of the area, the same things pop up: a brand-new pair of white socks underneath the bed, a tube of sunscreen left atop a neighboring cupboard, a T-shirt saturated with mud at the back of a cubby (it will not make the journey home).

The parents and campers are due at the *Waramaug* Indian Circle in about five minutes, and preparations for the final circle of the session are well under way, with benches from the dining hall provided for the extra attendees.

The families make their way over, filling the benches as a growing flame begins to punctuate the center of the circle. Suddenly, as inevitably seems to happen in crowds like this, there is an instant—perhaps a full second—where all the conversations magically come to a halt. Now it's the crackling fire that's doing the talking. Aaron Lewis pauses in the silence and stands to welcome everyone.

The staffmen will take turns announcing the awards and giving out the collection of certificates, ribbons, and symbolic citations. Staffmen can give out "K's," symbolizing technical mastery, and they can award certificates and ribbons to campers whose participation and enthusiasm were notable.

Next come the awards for ultimate Frisbee. Two kids who can throw the Frisbee the best are recognized, and then the staffman begins a short speech about a camper who might not have been the best at playing the game but who worked hard and improved drastically throughout the summer, especially on defense. He says that this is as important as throwing the Frisbee or being able to leap high to catch the disk, and it merits a ribbon for this camper. He pauses for dramatic effect, then announces the camper's name. It's Pepe.

When Pepe's name—to his complete shock—is called out in front of the entire wigwam, and the parents, and his own mother, Pepe's reaction is completely spontaneous. As he walks up to collect his ribbon, his already infectious smile is on high voltage. His eyes are smiling; his ears are smiling; his nose is smiling; his whole tiny body is a giant smile. It's just a small ribbon, but you get the feeling that as he clutches it in his right hand and sits back down next to his beaming mother, the ribbon will be making the journey back to Orange County amid heavy security.

From there, the awards ceremony morphs into the Q

Spratley show. Last night at the staff meeting in the dining hall, some of the biggest disagreements sprang from the dilemma of which awards to give Q. A ribbon in basketball was a given, but there were a host of other activities that he had quickly mastered this summer. His name is called again and again tonight—a "K" in diving, with the staffman who's making the announcement recalling a lesson one afternoon when Q was the one giving *him* pointers; a ribbon in mountaineering; a "K" in boxing, with Cameron MacDonald, who runs the program, recounting Q's awesome sparring sessions.

On each trip to the front, Q's head is cocked slightly sideways, his face passive yet struggling to contain emotion. On two of his trips, he actually skips and half-runs back to his spot on the bench, each time sneaking a quick glance at his mother to make sure he gets a look at her face.

While Q is busy racking up awards, Pepe has become the most vibrant camper. With each award called, the throng breaks out in cheers and Pepe's high-pitched screams can be heard above the crowd. A little while later, Pepe is called up again. The staffman announcing the soccer awards says, "This feisty young *Waramauge*r is known for his pizzazz."

Now he has a ribbon for each hand.

As the fire dims, the mood changes.

Aaron Lewis is suddenly talking about procedures for

campers leaving in the morning—or those leaving tonight. Now he's talking about the strangers who will join the tents tomorrow afternoon, the second-session campers. And then he's dismissing the group, which, not surprisingly, doesn't hurry to leave the benches, lingering instead around the fire, in part to stay warm, but also to preserve the magic of the Indian Circle that they just created. Like everything else in camp, the campfire has ended with a song. The lyric to this particular song of eighty years— "Now the day is over, Night is drawing nigh"—always triggers a bit of sadness. On this night, the last night of the summer, there is a more emotional overtone. The song ends with "Dunmore no more." It gets you, even at eight years of age. For now, a flame has been extinguished. Only next summer will there be Dunmore more . . . and more . . . and more.

Pepe and Q trudge back to their tents, the last time this summer they'll trace their steps along this route. Their mothers follow behind, talking like veterans as they rave about the campfire to each other. Maybe they're thinking about what might be going through the minds of their sons on the eve of the trip back across the country.

Oh Keewaydin, good night . . . God bring thee sweet dreams . . .

Oh Keewaydin, good night . . . may thy slumber be blessed . . .

There's something incredibly poignant about the words that Russ MacDonald is singing, standing near the backstop of *Waramaug* ball field, and then walking toward the wigwam's tents as he sings. Russ, *Waramaug's* director emeritus, sings this good-night song, the first of two each night that are sung to the campers directly after lights-out. His voice is a smooth tenor, a steady and slightly gravelly tone that projects to the farthest tents.

Pepe and Q have said their good-byes. With their flights back to California in the early morning tomorrow, the mothers determined that it made more sense to have the kids sleep with them tonight in the hotel. The good-byes were a bit awkward—high fives or half-hugs, imitating athletes on television. Pepe sought out a few basketball mates; Q stayed near his tent, almost avoiding the issue as his mom gently reminded him to say good-bye to Grant, his staffman.

Suddenly, they have vanished into the darkness. Keewaydin is made for coming, not for leaving, and the two boys from Orange County, a million miles from home, slipped away. I wonder if, on Route 70 on the way back to Middlebury, Pepe and Q suddenly feel like home is three thousand miles away from Keewaydin—rather than the opposite. Their beds are empty, the camp-issued linens still neatly placed on top of the cots, undisturbed from this morning's cleanup.

Out on *Waramaug* ball field, the sky is full of stars. A few staffmen lie down on the ground, eyes pinned upward. Meanwhile, Russ MacDonald pulls his recorder out of a pouch, and Carolyn Sotir, a former soprano in college, joins him as she does each night now for the second *Waramaug* good-night song.

Good night, Keewaydin, good night to you . . .
Sleep tight, Keewaydin, the whole night through . . .
The stars are shining with light so bright . . .
So good night, Keewaydin, good night . . .

About twenty feet away, Laurie Hare walks with Waboos carefully around the trees and onto the ball field. He's got one of his sweaters on, bundled to stay warm as the breeze cools the night.

Sweet dreams, Keewaydin, sweet dreams to you . . .

Sweet dreams, Keewaydin, that take you the whole night through . . .

Pepe and Q are probably getting close to Middlebury Inn by now, passing the darkened A&W where they had their first Vermont meal. They've had this song sung to them nearly every night for the past four weeks. But camp is over. The song is probably out of their heads, their minds now on an exciting night with their moms in a hotel.

You'll wake afresh with the morning light . . .

In the morning, they won't be at Keewaydin, but perhaps Keewaydin will be with them as they board their planes headed back west. Perhaps Keewaydin will remain with them all year. Perhaps, as it does with me, for the rest of their lives.

So good night, Keewaydin, good night . . .

On this July night in 2002, at 9:43 P.M., one month and seventeen days before his eighty-eighth birthday, Waboos stands at the heart of the camp, on *Waramaug* ball field. Today, like all days for him as he approaches the completion of his ninth decade of life, he couldn't see in the light, but right now, in a dark night under a layer of stars, he can see all right. He can sense exactly what's going on in front of him, what's going on behind him; what went on today at his camp, and what will go on tomorrow; how he got here, and, I hope, how he'll always be here, in some form or another, forever.

camp

Good night, good night.

The song ends. There are a few quiet moments of con-
templation, and then life goes on. Tomorrow there will be
airport check-ins for the kids going home. Tomorrow is
also the first day of camp for one hundred new campers,
replacing the ones who have left. They will begin the
process of learning and growing, laughing and playing, at
Keewaydin again.

epilogue

skills forever

Everybody paddles through pleasures in their lives: marriage, success, and children. And everybody paddles through storms as well, facing economic difficulties, fighting off adversaries, stumbling through unpleasant relationships, struggling with disease, moving on from a death in the family. How one deals with such disruptions in life, how one finds the strength to get through those times, how one perseveres is a mark of who that person is. And a person finds his oars—his tools to get through—early on, during early childhood development, in the formative days of life. Early education—and early play—is important. Summer camp is where the tools to fend off the hard times are acquired. They are tools that have worked for generations of campers, and they will work forever.

Camp grabs hold of you when you're young, the kind of home you at once claim as your own but also share, share with the kid in the cot next to you and share with the venerable staffman who's been there longer than you've been alive. It's one of America's ultimate communal dwellings, a shared experience and anchor of stories that campers young and old exchange far from our camps, long after we've spent our last night in a tent or cabin. Camp is a laboratory for safe danger, and the science practiced in this lab will never be outdated. It's God and humans teaming up to provide nature's ultimate playground, where survival in the woods becomes an exercise in training for life's real-world, man-made challenges; where young people can develop their physical and natural skills while also maturing and growing socially.

Over the past few summers, like me, my father, and my sons, Pepe and Q have acquired their tools for life at Keewaydin. This summer, the summer of 2005, will be their fourth summer as campers. At Keewaydin, the fourth summer is a real milestone, as campers who've been at camp this long are inducted as *Papoosiwogs,* or old-timers. It's an honor meant to single out those who have spent time learning at camp, but really it's also an honor society that Keewaydin would eagerly brag of. It is out of the ranks of the *Papoosiwogs* that the finest of Keewaydin emerge to face the world. They've spent the most time there, been on the most trips, experienced the most adversity, had the most initiative, shown the most commitment.

Pepe has done all this without physically growing much—he's still seriously undersized for a young teenager. He's just as excitable, but if you look at his eyes closely, you can tell he's grown a bit inside. He's seen more of the world, not only at Keewaydin, where he's been a part of some classic canoe trips, but also back home in Anaheim, where some of his peers have begun a descent into gangs and drugs. When it's the older kids, it's easy to just say no; when it's the kids you've played with after school in the street for years, it's more complicated. Even in winters, when I've seen him during California Keewaydin re-unions, his enthusiasm for Keewaydin is potent, his command of the camp's language as fresh as it would be in Vermont in the middle of July. Camp, his mother tells a Spanish-speaking translator, is where Pepe has found the individuality and initiative to steer clear of trouble so far in his neighborhood.

Q remains the distant, easygoing youngster he was in his first summer at Keewaydin, but his focus on organized sports has waned a bit outside camp. Maybe it's because the sports are too easy for such a natural young athlete, or, conversely, because the commitment to practice is too great for a kid whose focus wanders easily; his latest interests are motor scooters and motorbikes. He starred in football and hockey for school and neighborhood teams a few years ago, but has lost the drive to commit for now. Keewaydin, then, has become a place of stability for Q, where he returns to the basketball court, the climbing rocks, and the canoe.

It's incredibly striking to see Pepe and Q in their native Orange County, amid the threats from drugs and gangs. They, like all kids there, appear very vulnerable, at one moment puffing out their chests to assert themselves in a threatening environment, and then, in the middle of ordering fast food, reminding a visitor how small, vulnerable, and young they are as they debate the merits of getting vanilla or strawberry shakes. At Keewaydin, there are no such contradictions; here, they are boys among boys, in the laboratory that has produced so many great men.

And at camp, the man who's melded so many Pepes and Qs over decades and decades is still in his cottage. Waboos is ninety years old now. He carefully moves through camp with the aid of a rolling walker; perhaps a wooden cane would be more romantic, but this is safer amid the roots and stones of the campus. It's his latest way to deal with old age, his latest trick to keep himself mobile, his latest tool for life. His vision hasn't improved, but somehow he still looks you in the eye when he makes a point. And inside, his mind's eye, the one that really counts, is still virile and strong, still the source of pointed questions about my work and my book, in a genial tone that still commands respect and a straight answer.

His wife has now passed away, at the nursing home in Philadelphia. There was a quiet service at the end of summer, and, appropriately, a flower bed at Keewaydin had been dedicated to her memory. Waboos's life is now fully anchored at the camp, his calendar solely oriented toward those two magical months when the place he has kept afloat for so many years gives him renewed energy, increased vigor, the world beginning anew.

I've been up to camp each of the three summers since my son and I dropped off Pepe and Q that first day, nervous about whether the two wide-eyed boys from Orange County could adapt to the northeastern wilderness, and wondering whether the camp could help these street savvy pre-teens. Well, I think I'll find my answer this summer, when we drop off the sixteen kids from Southern California who now go to Keewaydin and Songadeewin on combined scholarship from our family's foundation and the General Breed scholarship program. Pepe and Q and Noelle and Veronica are the leaders of the pack, talking up the A&W on the plane ride east, and taking the youngest kids—this summer, nine-year-olds headed to *Annwi*—to their wigwams the first day.

And this summer, while Pepe and Q lead the way, and Waboos is mobbed by the campers and parents and alumni who descend upon his cottage, I'll slip away to take my own self-guided tour. They say time travel might never be possible, but I do it with each lap around Keewaydin, and each picture I see—the campers running around on the ball fields and in the lake, the staffmen milling about, overseeing the younger ones and enjoying their summer in such a special place. The sounds I hear, the smells I smell, the spots to stand to catch the perfect breeze on a steamy Vermont summer day—all the same as when I roamed here as a ten-year-old camper, a twenty-year-old staffman, a forty-year-old parent. In a world swept up in constant change and ever-fluctuating trends, obsessed with the moment and little else, Keewaydin is a treasured exception of stability. It hasn't changed. I fantasize that Pepe and Q a decade from now will be the staffmen at Keewaydin to my yet unborn grandchildren, and Waboos . . . Waboos will be a centenarian, somehow still meandering around the campus, "Hi, Mike," he'll say. "How's the family? How's John Angelo? Still playing tennis against him?"

michael d. eisner

Last summer, after spending a few days on Lake Dunmore, I felt an obligation to explore the Jamestown of camping. I decided to drag the kidnappable John Angelo, his wife, Judy, and Jane up to northern Ontario and Lake Temagami, five hundred miles northwest of Lake Dunmore, the site of the original Camp Keewaydin, the place where it all began, taking the same trip that Commodore Clark made over a century ago (albeit by plane, car, and motorboat, not canoe). It's an incredible place, with a pureness and freshness to it you won't soon forget. There are no cell phones up here to call Burbank in order to hear the latest drama on and off the stages, and no electricity, either. And much of Temagami is reminiscent of Dunmore—the traditions, the Algonquin words, even the smell of camp linens—two brothers separated at birth, now reunited. Temagami is exclusively a tripping camp—you don't need your baseball mitt, a basketball, or a tennis racket up there. Just a canoe.

At both my Keewaydin, on Lake Dunmore, and this Keewaydin, on Lake Temagami, it's about teamwork and friendships; the loyalty of your bunkmates; the protection and security provided by your staffmen; and the alternative universe of the outback wilderness. And as the four of us walk on a path on this secluded island in Canada, I realize that both camps are epitomized by one thing: the canoe. The canoe is another member of the cast at camp, just like the staffman you never forget, the boy in your bow, or Waboos. The canoe is the extension of your body in the watered wilderness. Moving you forward, it is your life preserver, and never sinks, carrying your food and your shelter. On a canoe trip a boy learns the value of the right equipment, the proper protection from the elements, the need for safety. Like memories of camp in the winter months, before a trip begins, your canoe just sits there, back on the lake, lying dormant. But when your trip starts, you reunite with your friend, your partner.

Fifty years ago, I'm on Raquette Lake in the Adirondack Mountains, five canoes moving through headwinds that just picked up, an unexpected storm—driving rain . . . whitecaps and a canoe fully loaded for the first day of the trip. I'm twelve years old and I'm in the stern, hardly able to communicate with my bowman and unable to see the other canoes. Finally a staffman's canoe comes into view and instructs us to head to shore immediately. Four canoes make it safely but mine does not. A massive wave hits us almost simultaneously with the loudest thunder strike I have ever heard. The wanagans quickly sink to the bottom. There goes the silver cake mix. My duffel bag floats. A tarp disappears. But my bowman and I hold on to the canoe, our support and our protection. There is no fear—well, maybe just a little—but we know what to do. We have been taught. Never leave the canoe. Go underneath if need be. Find the air pocket. Get on one side and paddle with your legs to shore.

And that day, we did, and we got to shore, which seemed like hundreds of yards away but was maybe only fifty. We lost some food. The staffmen went and got our duffels, and although we were wet and cold and shaken, we were feted and honored that night like heroes and dried and given soup and attention and a story to tell for the rest of our lives.

Today, no matter how daunting the task in front of me, I think of that canoe, that trip, that experience, that early education. I believe Pepe and Q will do the same. Today, no matter what's in front of me, I think of Waboos and I think of camp.

glossary of
keewaydin terms

Annwi **(n):** Wigwam for youngest campers (ages eight to nine).

Brown's Bay (n): Area of camp for staff and their families to live (next to *Wiantinaug* ball field).

Bug House (n): Building in lagoon area that houses nature artifacts and materials.

Bumwad (n): Toilet paper.

Carnival (n): An event at which campers make their own booths to celebrate the coming of midseason.

Corral (n): The relaxing area outside the dining hall on the edge of *Waramaug* ball field.

Coup (n): Earned by completing a certain level of achievement in one area of activity.

glossary

Dispensary (n): Nurse's office; sick house.

Elephant Bumwad (n): Paper towel.

Formation (n): Daily saluting of the flag, typically done in the morning.

Fort (n): Bathroom.

Four Winds Ceremony (n): At the beginning of the summer, a ceremony where the four winds gather at a campfire with the whole camp.

Friday Frolic (n): Weekly show featuring skits performed by campers; takes place on Friday nights.

Garboon (n): Garbage can.

Glick (n): Lunchtime drink; comes in four flavors.

Gong (n): Circular length of old railroad track that is rung to call people to meals.

Guzzle (n): End-of-trip treat; frequently done at McDonald's or A&W.

Hare House (n): Small cabin home to camp archives and Waboos's office.

glossary

Indian Circle (n): Gathering within each wigwam each morning and afternoon, in which activities are chosen for the day; where campfires are held.

Inspection (n): Daily checking of tent/cabin cleanliness.

Inwigo **(n):** Ladies' bathroom.

Kicker **(n):** Camp newspaper read aloud at Sunday-night campfire.

Moosalamoo **(n):** Wigwam for oldest campers (ages fourteen and fifteen); also name of the mountain overlooking camp.

Multihouse (n): Camp theater.

Old-Timer (n): Title given to those who have been at Keewaydin for four or more years.

Papoosiwog **(n):** Name for those in their fourth year at camp.

Portage (n, v): The carrying of canoes and equipment from one body of water to another on a canoe trip; the act of carrying the canoes.

Songadeewin (n): Literally meaning strong of heart, name of girls camp.

glossary

Staff Brat (n): Child of staff who is too young to be a camper.

Sunday Circle (n): Camp gathering on Sundays where people share thoughts and musical talents.

Sunset Arena (n): Boxing and wrestling ring beyond *Waramaug* ball field along Keewaydin Road.

Temagami (n): The original Keewaydin camp in Canada, recently reconnected to Dunmore through the Keewaydin Foundation.

Wallop (v): To wash dishes, etc., on trips.

Wanagan (n): A large box in which trip supplies are carried.

***Waramaug* (n):** Wigwam for ten- and eleven-year-old campers.

Wet Loaders (n): Old sneakers used for canoeing.

***Wiantinaug* (n):** Wigwam for twelve- and thirteen-year-old campers.

Wigwam (n): Unit of campers, organized by age.

about the author

Michael D. Eisner has worked in the entertainment industry for over forty years, the last twenty-one as chief executive officer of The Walt Disney Company. Before that, he was a camper and staffman at Camp Keewaydin in Salisbury, Vermont, for nine summers. He and his wife, Jane, live in Los Angeles. Their three sons, all former Keewaydin campers themselves, live nearby. All of his proceeds from this book have been donated to The Eisner Foundation, which is providing scholarships to send underserved children to the camp.

The author with present-day Keewaydin campers Q Spratley (left) and Pepe Molina (right).